A CENTURY OF MAN-MADE DISASTERS

A CENTURY OF MAN-MADE DISASTERS

NIGEL BLUNDELL

PEN & SWORD HISTORY

First published in Great Britain in 2019 by
PEN & SWORD HISTORY
An imprint of
Pen & Sword Books Ltd
47 Church Street
Barnsley
South Yorkshire
S70 2AS

ISBN 978-1-52674-868-3

Typeset by Concept, Huddersfield, West Yorkshire, HD4 5JL.
Printed and bound in India by Replika Press Pvt. Ltd.

Pen & Sword Books Limited incorporates the imprints of Atlas, Archaeology, Aviation, Discovery, Family History, Fiction, History, Maritime, Military, Military Classics, Politics, Select, Transport, True Crime, Air World, Frontline Publishing, Leo Cooper, Remember When, Seaforth Publishing, The Praetorian Press, Wharncliffe Local History, Wharncliffe Transport, Wharncliffe True Crime and White Owl.

For a complete list of Pen & Sword titles please contact
PEN & SWORD BOOKS LIMITED
47 Church Street, Barnsley, South Yorkshire S70 2AS, England
E-mail: enquiries@pen-and-sword.co.uk
Website: www.pen-and-sword.co.uk

Contents

Introduction

There is an enduring fascination with disasters, especially those that are man-made and, it seems, just waiting to happen. Perhaps it is because they remind us of our own mortality; that we too could be in the wrong place at the wrong time, the victims of someone else's error.

Who can say, after news of a plane disaster, that they haven't imagined themselves in a stricken aircraft, shuddering at the thought of the chaos, the panic and the certainty that death must be close?

In this book, the appalling carnage when two jumbo jets collided at Tenerife bears powerful witness to the horror of man-made tragedy. The story of the explosion aboard the Challenger space shuttle reveals how warnings that were ignored led to the deaths of seven astronauts. We recall the horrors of Aberfan, the Welsh village in which schoolchildren were buried alive. We report on the failings that caused the nuclear nightmare at Chernobyl, a poisonous blot on the face of the globe.

These and the other major calamities in this book took place in the twentieth century, a period during which the power and scale of industrialization changed the planet. An unforeseen consequence was the creation of more human-created catastrophes than ever before experienced.

There are, however, further links between these horrific events. They were all caused by either folly or greed, or both. Yet despite the tales of monstrous misfortune, many also produced heart-lifting stories of human resilience, selflessness, sacrifice and pure heroism.

So this book is indeed a catalogue of disaster. Yet its pages also recall the courage and spirit with which men and women face adversity ... and win through.

Chapter One

The 'Unsinkable' *Titanic* (1912)

The chunk of ice that sank the *Titanic* had been forming for 15,000 years. When it finally broke away from its polar glacier in the summer of 1909, it was a billion-tonne mega-berg. On its three-year voyage through the Arctic, down past the coast of Newfoundland and out into the busy Atlantic shipping lanes, it slowly melted, becoming more and more unpredictable.

By 12 April 1912, the iceberg was in the last few weeks of its existence. Battered by storms and reduced by constant weathering, it was by now highly unstable, rolling over every few days. However, it was still a significant obstacle: 500,000 tons of ice compared with the 'mere' 52,310 tons of steel of the world's largest passenger ship steaming straight towards it.

RMS *Titanic* was the largest man-made moving object on earth and her owners proclaimed: 'God himself could not sink this ship.' Who could have believed otherwise as she sped across the Atlantic on her maiden voyage, her bands playing, her ballrooms filled, her barmen preparing the most elaborate cocktails and her chefs the most succulent dishes. The cream of British and American society were enjoying

RMS *Titanic* was not only the world's largest passenger ship but the largest moving object on earth.

The *Titanic* under construction at Belfast's Harland and Wolff shipyard.

the voyage of a lifetime, among them American businessman John Jacob Astor IV, the richest man aboard; fellow financier and philanthropist Benjamin Guggenheim; Isidor Straus, co-owner of Macy's department store; fashion designer Lady Duff-Gordon; painter Francis Millet; and the now-infamous Joseph Bruce Ismay, managing director of the *Titanic*'s owners, the White Star Line.

For these first-class passengers, there was unparalleled luxury. The *Titanic* enjoyed the first shipboard swimming pool and a crane to load and unload limousines. The elite could avail themselves of Arabian-style Turkish baths, a gym, a squash court, a lounge modelled on a room at Versailles, a Parisian café and a palm court. There were sumptuous suites and cabins for the fortunate 735 first-class passengers, but lesser cabins for the further 1,650 passengers booked in second and third class.

After the pomp and partying of her departure from Southampton, the *Titanic* had stopped briefly at the French port of Cherbourg and then at Queenstown (now Cobh), Cork, before, on the evening of Thursday, 11 April, heading out into the Atlantic. The liner sliced easily through the calm waters, the huge turbines driving her forward at a 'full speed ahead' of 21.5 knots. The 2,000-plus passengers and crew were secure in the knowledge that the liner boasted not only luxury beyond belief but state-of-the-art safety measures. The hull was double-bottomed in the unlikely event that it might hit an iceberg. It had fifteen transverse bulkheads running the length of the vessel to isolate incoming water in the unthinkable possibility of it springing a leak.

In the light of these safety measures, the owners of the *Titanic*, the White Star Line, had deemed it unnecessary to carry sufficient lifeboats to cater for all the passengers and crew, and the lifeboats carried were designed only to ferry people to nearby rescue vessels, not to bear everyone on board simultaneously. In fact, the sixteen lifeboats, it was later calculated, would have held just one-quarter of the passengers and crew. After all, who would ever need them?

During the morning of 14 April the temperature dropped suddenly and the captain, Edward Smith, was warned by his radio operators that there were icebergs in

Titanic leaves Southampton at the start of her maiden transatlantic voyage.

The liner's top deck, showing the inadequate number of lifeboats.

the region. The *Titanic*, however, did not reduce speed; there was the promised prestige of an award-winning, swift passage to America with a welcoming committee waiting in New York.

Shortly before midnight, the lookout shouted: 'Iceberg right ahead.' The bridge ordered 'Hard a-port' but it was too late. As the bow of the ship began to swing to port, the iceberg scraped along her starboard side below the water line. There was barely a jolt to disturb the partying passengers or wake those who had retired to their cabins. According to one of the survivors, the crash 'sounded like tearing a strip off a piece of calico, nothing more. Later it grew in intensity, as though someone had drawn a giant finger along the side of the ship.'

As the officers on the bridge watched the dim shape of the iceberg slip away to their stern, Captain Smith, who had been relaxing elsewhere in the ship, raced to his post. He arrived on the bridge as the first officer was ordering: 'Stop engines.' Smith sent below for damage reports and could hardly believe his ears when he was told that a huge rent had been torn down the side of the liner. Water was pouring in at an alarming

Captain Edward Smith failed to reduce speed despite iceberg warnings, for which he paid with his life.

rate and the watertight bulkheads, in which so much faith had been placed, were now breached. The greatest passenger liner the world had ever seen was sinking.

Throughout the drama being enacted high on the bridge, the liner's passengers were blissfully unaware of the peril they were facing. So gentle had been the collision that few of them had even commented on it. Some of the more energetic wandered onto the open decks and picked up bits of ice to freshen their glasses of whisky. One group even began a 'snowball' fight with debris that had been blown off the passing iceberg.

Captain Smith was a highly-experienced skipper. He reacted calmly to the knowledge that a death knell had been sounded for the liner with which he had been entrusted. He ordered the radio room to put out distress calls. Later he had the lifeboats uncovered and made ready.

The passengers in superior accommodation were raised from their slumbers by apologetic knocks on their cabin doors and, as they arrived bleary-eyed on deck, the lifeboats were swung out and the order passed down the line: 'Women and children first'. Only then, as the captain ordered distress rockets to be launched, was there the first hint of panic among the passengers. It spread swiftly to the lower decks, where the greatest tragedy on board that night befell the 670 immigrants in third class, or steerage, who were trapped below decks behind doors kept locked by order of the US Immigration Department. By the time they eventually battered their way to the outside, most of the lifeboats had slipped from their davits.

Even the crew was in a state of confusion, never having performed a full boat drill during sea trials. They failed to find many of the collapsible life-rafts, which had been stowed in inaccessible places, and even when uncovered, they did not know how to assemble them.

Meanwhile, the radio operators had alerted two other liners to the *Titanic*'s plight: the *Frankfurt* and the *Carpathia*. The captain of the latter was so incredulous at the news that the 'unsinkable' *Titanic* was in trouble that he twice asked his radio operators whether they had got the message right. When assured that they had, and believing that his vessel was closest to the *Titanic*, he ordered his engine room to speed to the rescue.

The *Carpathia*, however, was all of 60 miles from the stricken ship. Much closer was another liner, the *California*, which was only 19 miles from the *Titanic*. Aboard the *California*, the *Titanic*'s distress flares had been seen by crewmen, who had reported them to the bridge. Astonishingly, they were told that they must either be celebratory rockets or a false alarm. The *California*'s skipper, Stanley Lord, insisted until his dying day that his ship had not seen the *Titanic* and that he could not have arrived in time to save lives. He admitted in evidence to the subsequent inquiry that rockets had been sighted but that they were taken to be company signals.

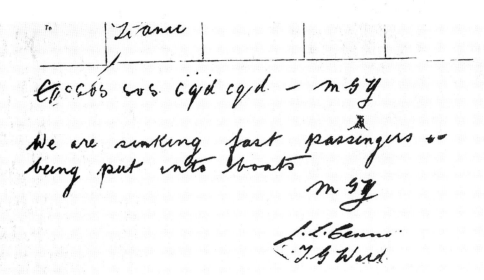

The SOS message sent out by the stricken ship's radio operators.

So, as the *California* remained stationary, the *Titanic* slowly sank. It was now around 2.00am and the bow was beginning to dip lower in the calm but freezing black North Atlantic. The lifeboats, which had been filled but not lowered in the hope of rescue, were now sent down to the icy waters below. Because many wives had refused to leave their husbands, many of the lifeboats were only half-full.

Among the many human dramas that night was the stoicism of Isidor Straus's wife Ida who refused the offer of a place in a lifeboat and died in her husband's arms. Fellow millionaire Benjamin Guggenheim and his valet Victor Giglio dressed in evening clothes to meet their Maker 'like gentlemen'. The White Star Line's cowardly boss, Bruce Ismay, showed no such courage and jumped into a lifeboat, thereafter forever condemning himself to a life of ignominy.

One of the ship's bands struck up *Nearer, My God, to Thee* and the reassuring sound wafted across the black sea as the weeping women in the lifeboats watched their menfolk waving farewell from the decks high above them.

At 2.30am Captain Smith, having now realized that no other vessel was coming to his aid, ordered: 'Abandon ship!' The *Titanic* was at an almost 90-degree angle in the ocean, her lights still twinkling and reflecting on the lifeboats drifting away from the final horror shortly to come. As if wanting to escape their inevitable fate for just a few seconds longer, some of those who had not got into the lifeboats scrambled up the decks like mountaineers to reach the doomed ship's stern, pointing upwards like a skyscraper. Then she went down.

There was a rumble of machinery crashing from stern to bow, then a hissing and bubbling as the boilers exploded. As the *Titanic* descended through 13,000ft of water, a giant vortex was created which sucked debris and bodies into the depths. Those in

How the sinking was depicted in James Cameron's 1997 blockbuster movie which, with a budget of $200 million, cost more than the real ship.

the water who were not dragged down by the whirlpool did not drown; they died of cold within two minutes of hitting the freezing water. On the surface, newly-widowed women wept in the bitterly cold night air.

At 4.00am the *Carpathia* arrived and took aboard all those in the lifeboats. Only later did the final dreadful accounting take place. Perplexingly, the death toll remains inexact; so too do the passenger numbers because not all those issued with tickets actually made the voyage. Also, fortuitously as it turned out, the liner was carrying only half her full capacity of 2,435 as it was low season and shipping from the UK had been disrupted by a coal-mining strike.

(**Left**) Millionaire Benjamin Guggenheim and his valet donned evening dress 'to die like gentlemen'. (**Centre**) Fellow millionaire Isidor Straus and his wife Ida, who refused a place in a lifeboat and died with her husband. (**Right**) White Star Line boss Bruce Ismay showed no such courage and joined women and children in a lifeboat.

Lifeboats from the *Titanic* approach the rescue ship *Carpathia*.

The scale of the disaster is revealed on the streets of London ... Worried relatives wait for news posted outside the White Star Line's offices in London.

According to official British figures at the time, there were 711 survivors from a total number of 2,201 crew and passengers, which would have meant a death toll of 1,490. The figures have since been revised with estimates of up to 2,224 aboard, which could mean a death toll as high as 1,635. However, nowadays it is generally reported that 'more than 1,500' perished, including approximately 815 of the passengers.

Yet need ANY of them have died? A century after her demise, the question was still being asked: who was to blame for the death of the *Titanic*? Now viewed as a testimony to man's flawed ambition and proud folly, fascination in the subject has never waned, fuelled by books, movies and fresh discoveries about the liner's last voyage, perhaps the most revealing being the discovery in 1985 of the ship's last resting place.

The *Titanic* had lain undisturbed in her watery grave for seventy-three years when in July 1985 American oceanographer Dr Robert Ballard led an undersea team which found her, broken up into three pieces and partly shattered by the water pressure on her descent. In a 5,000ft debris field lay the artefacts of a lost age, from intact wine bottles to expensive toiletries to ceramic dolls of child passengers. One of the most poignant images captured by Ballard's cameras was of a broken lifeboat davit, hanging limply on the edge of the ship.

This and further submarine expeditions to the wreck reignited the debate about who or what was to blame for the sinking. The ship's construction, the lack of lifeboats and the speed maintained through an iceberg area were all well-argued causes.

The bow of the *Titanic* as discovered in 1985 lying 13,000ft deep at the bottom of the ocean.

However, in 2006 another theory was raised suggesting that despite all of the above, the *Titanic* need never have sunk and that the most notorious maritime disaster of all time was a needless loss of 1,500 lives.

A fresh study of the collision showed that the scale of the tragedy was all down to the way the crew handled the unfolding drama as the liner raced towards her fate, for their biggest mistake was not colliding with an iceberg but trying to avoid it. If the *Titanic* had hit the iceberg head-on she would have survived but, by trying to steer around it, her fate was sealed. The world's leading expert on iceberg collisions, Claude Daley, a specialist in ice and ship engineering at Memorial University in Newfoundland, said:

> It was perfectly natural that the crew tried to avoid the iceberg but it was absolutely the wrong thing to do. Had the *Titanic* held its course and hit head-on, the ship would have come to a shuddering stop. The bow would have been crushed and crumpled, flooding only one part of the ship that no passenger ever entered, but that would have acted as a buffer and cushioned the impact. Sure, people would have been knocked over, the china would have broken and there would have been quite a mess — but afterwards they would have cleaned up, sealed off the forepeak (bow area), and continued on their way. They would have got home again.

The actual iceberg that sank the *Titanic*. This photograph was taken by the chief steward of the German ship *Prinz Adalbert*, just a few miles south of the disaster site.

That is not what happened, of course. When the iceberg was spotted, the crew on the bridge tried to steer around it, which had the effect of slewing the liner across the side of the berg. To compound the error, in their panic the crew also ordered the engines to go into reverse, which was a totally contradictory action. As revealed in a 2006 BBC TV investigation titled *The Iceberg that Sank the Titanic*, the liner's relatively small rudder needed a high-speed flow of water around it to enable it to steer effectively. The combination of the avoiding action and the propellers churning in reverse ensured that the collision would become a catastrophe as steel and ice collided side-on.

In a footnote to history, although the *Titanic* was doomed, the iceberg survived, albeit not for long. A photograph was taken of it by the chief steward of the German ship *Prinz Adalbert* a few miles south of where the *Titanic* had sunk. News of the disaster had not reached him, and he snapped the picture because he noticed a mysterious 'great scar of red paint' that ran along the berg's base, suggesting a recent collision with a ship.

However, the warm Gulf Stream was already eating voraciously into the iceberg and barely a week or two after the *Titanic*'s demise, the last piece of the killer berg disappeared into the Atlantic. Thus, not far from the liner's rusting hulk, there must be a scattering of soil where the last of the 15,000-year-old iceberg's rocky sediments were finally released onto the ocean bed.

Chapter Two

Five-Train Catastrophe (1915)

The dawn of 22 May 1915 instilled a mixed sense of sadness, fear and excitement in the young soldiers. That morning they clambered onto a troop train in Scotland for the long journey south. Ahead lay the trenches and battlefields of the First World War and the prospect of dying for their country. For some of the fresh-faced youths it was their first venture outside Scotland. Tragically, for many it would also be their last. They would die sooner than their bleakest nightmares predicted: among 500 dead and injured in what was Britain's worst-ever train wreck.

The incident occurred only a few minutes' ride from the Scottish border at the remote Quintinshill signal box near Gretna Green. There, two crashes involved five trains: the troop train, a local passenger train, an express train and two freights. In the inferno that followed, the soldiers died horribly, most of them slowly burned to death. Civilian men, women and children died too.

Since described as a 'Titanic moment' in the history of rail travel, the disaster was caused by complacency. At the time, the blame fell almost entirely on two supposedly careless, rule-breaking signalmen, who were jailed for criminal negligence. However, it has since been argued that the pair were made scapegoats to get railway bosses and the government off the hook. For the antiquated troop train, its lighting powered by gas cylinders beneath the floors, was a travelling time-bomb that should have been scrapped years previously, and the timetable for its journey south required near-impossible speeds.

The route to catastrophe began when the soldiers of the Royal Scots' 7th (Leith) Battalion boarded their troop train 'Special' at Larbet Station, near Falkirk. From there its destination in England was top secret. Spies, the soldiers had been told, were everywhere. In fact, they were headed for an English port to be shipped across the Mediterranean to fight at Gallipoli.

The 'Special' was due to travel past the signal box at Quintinshill and on across the English-Scottish border to Carlisle. Northbound express traffic that morning was running late. Both the 11.45 London Euston to Edinburgh sleeper and the midnight Euston to Glasgow sleeper had fallen half an hour behind schedule. They were not

The scene of carnage. (**Above**) Blazing carriages following a five-train pile-up near the England-Scotland border in what remains Britain's worst-ever rail disaster. (**Below**) Fire hoses play on a burned-out sleeping car.

expected to pull out of Carlisle station until 5.50am and 6.05am respectively, even though the drivers would be pushing their locomotives hard to make up time. The London and North-Western Railway took great pride in its punctuality. So did the Caledonian Railway, which ran an all-stations 'slow local' between Carlisle and Beattock using the same northbound line as the expresses pounding up from London. Affectionately known among locals as 'the *Parley*', this train was due to leave Carlisle at 6.10am and reach Beattock by 7.49am to make a connection.

If the sleepers were on time, the arrangement went without a hitch. If they were late, as they so often were, the *Parley* had to be held back to ensure the line north was clear. In recent months, Caledonian officials had found a way around this conundrum by starting the *Parley* off ahead of the London trains and then shunting it into sidings at Quintinshill to let them pass. This manoeuvre had been taking place on average once a week for the past six months.

This was a convenient arrangement for signalmen James Tinsley and George Meakin, who manned the Quintinshill box on a shift system. Usually they had to walk the mile and a half to work from Gretna, where they both lived. However, on mornings when the *Parley* was to be sidelined, one of them could get a ride on the footplate and jump off when the train stopped at the signal box. All they had to do was check with the Gretna signalman beforehand to find out whether the London trains were on time.

There was one snag with this piece of rule-bending. Tinsley and Meakin were supposed to swap shifts at 6.00am, although the *Parley* never got to Quintinshill before 6.13am. This meant that the handover was always later than it should have been. To cover this up, the signal box's log book was manipulated to give the impression that the day man had arrived on time at 6.00am. This was craftily achieved by the night man entering no further information in the train register after 6.00am and instead logging any entries for the next quarter of an hour on a separate sheet of paper. The day-shift man would then copy the entries into the register as soon as he arrived. The aim was to deceive any nosey official who might check the register. From 6.00am every day the handwriting would always alter: supposed 'proof' that the changeover had taken place according to the rules.

At 6.10am on 22 May, Tinsley, who was on the day shift, boarded the *Parley* at Gretna, heading for Quintinshill where he would belatedly join Meakin in the signal box at the end of his night shift. Normally Tinsley would dismount when the train had diverted into the Quintinshill northbound siding. However, when the *Parley* reached the relevant set of points it became clear this was impossible. A goods train had been shunted onto the siding to await collection and there was no room to fit in the *Parley* as well.

Tinsley decided he would have to direct the *Parley* off the northbound line and onto the main southbound track until the two London-Scotland services had passed.

This was not a particularly unusual or dangerous operation. It had been accomplished four times in the last six months with no problems. The most important thing was for the signal box immediately north of Quintinshill, at Kirkpatrick, to be kept informed.

At 6.38am the Edinburgh-bound express passed safely, but soon afterwards the situation took a more complex twist when a southbound goods train pulling empty coal wagons turned up. The driver was ordered into the southbound siding to await instructions.

To summarize, the sight from the Quintinshill box was now as follows. Northbound siding: goods train. Northbound main line: clear. Southbound main line: *Parley* train. Southbound siding: empty coal train.

Tinsley was by now in the signal box, copying Meakin's notes into the train register. Meakin had stayed on for a few moments to read his colleague's newspaper and talk about the progress of the war. Some time in the next few minutes, one of the pair (though both later denied it) sent a message to the Kirkpatrick box advising that the coal train had been shunted off the southbound main line. Crucially, that message made no mention of the fact that the *Parley* train had now been shunted on to it. Tinsley and Meakin had also failed to pull the levers controlling the southbound track into their protective collars. This would have provided a visible reminder to them that the line could not be used. The die for disaster was now cast.

At 6.42am Kirkpatrick offered Quintinshill control of the troop train. Tinsley accepted it and pulled all the southbound levers to show the line ahead was free. Hardly had he returned to his copying when Gretna offered him the late-running Glasgow express. Again Tinsley agreed to take it under his control and pulled all northbound signals to the 'clear' position. Meanwhile the *Parley* sat on the southbound line, brakes locked, a doomed train awaiting destruction.

A minute later, the troop 'Special', travelling down a 1:200 line gradient, rounded the curve into Quintinshill and cannoned into the *Parley* at 70mph. The impact had a devastating effect on the soldiers' carriages, squashing them from a total length of 237 yards down to 67 yards. Both trains were now a jumble of broken coaches, many of which had spilled onto the northbound express track.

Minutes later the Glasgow-bound express, topping 60mph, smashed into the wreckage, which then spilled out onto the stationary freights stored in the passing loops. Gas from the underfloor cylinders of the troop train's old wooden carriages ignited, starting a fire that engulfed the shattered train, together with a sleeping car near the front of the express.

The exact death toll will probably never be known. Wartime restrictions on information meant that the full horror of the pile-up was suppressed and official figures claimed an unlikely 215 soldiers dead and 191 injured. The casualty list is also uncertain because so many bodies were burned beyond recognition and the roll of the battalion was destroyed in the blaze. What is known is that of the 500 soldiers

(**Above**) Wrecked carriage of a local train, with the undamaged locomotive of a coal train in the background. (**Below**) Locals raced to the scene to tend the injured after the crash at Quintinshill, near Gretna Green.

(**Above**) Bodies lie under blankets and rugs in a field. The barn at the back also served as a makeshift mortuary.
(**Below**) The engine of the London-Glasgow express with, in front of it, the troop train tender.

Funeral procession carrying the dead of the 7th Royal Scots through the streets of Edinburgh.

on the train, only 58 men and 7 officers were present for roll-call at 4.00pm that afternoon.

However, a recent book investigating the catastrophe put the death toll at 230, including four unidentified women and children, and the total of injured at 246. Published in 2013 by Pen & Sword, *The Quintinshill Conspiracy: The Shocking True Story Behind Britain's Worst Rail Disaster* claimed that a company cover-up began immediately after the disaster. Co-authors Adrian Searle and Jack Richards, who studied the crash over several years, accused the rail company of a cynical whitewash and manipulation of evidence at the public inquiry, which lasted just one day, and at subsequent hearings. They conceded that the signalmen did break company rules but claimed that these transgressions were not in themselves sufficient to cause the catastrophic five-train collision.

A local newspaper published this picture of signalman George Meakin following the crash.

Meakin had left to his colleague the task of safeguarding the local train, temporarily parked on the 'wrong' line, yet it was alleged that Tinsley somehow 'forgot' about the train on which he had just arrived. The book suggests Tinsley had in fact suffered an epileptic seizure and uncovers a statement by his doctor confirming that the signalman was prone

(**Left**) James Tinsley (*centre*) arrives for the initial brief public inquiry. (**Right**) Some of the injured were also called to the inquiry in Carlisle.

James Tinsley (*left*) with his lawyer at the crash site.

to fits; not something his employer would care to be made public. The Caledonian Railway faced further embarrassment because it had insisted on maintaining peacetime express train schedules, despite the greatly increased demands of wartime traffic. The book also revealed that rule-breaking and lax supervisory control was prevalent on the Caledonian network. It would have been politically damaging if Prime Minister Herbert Asquith's Liberal government had been found guilty of consigning British soldiers to a potential death-trap.

According to author Searle: 'The Government's Railway Executive had effectively condemned the Royal Scots to ride in antiquated carriages at express train speeds for which they were never designed. Worse, the vehicles were lit by those gas cylinders beneath the floors – a tinderbox on wheels.' Searle even believes that the signalmen may have been paid for going along with the cover-up: 'It appears that, in exchange for Tinsley's health problems being kept out of the picture, his family would be looked after by the company during and after his imprisonment. In Meakin's case, the probability is that he was financially compensated.'

Both men were re-employed after serving their sentences, Tinsley being jailed for three years and Meakin for eighteen months. 'They were scapegoats,' says Searle, 'the easiest of kills. And with the pair receiving their supposed just deserts, both the company and national government were kept free of damaging censure.'

A memorial erected at Gretna Green in 1995 to the memory of the dead at Quintinshill.

Chapter Three

Brought Down by Pride (1930)

British airship R101, the largest flying machine in the world, more than 700ft long and filled with 5 million cubic feet of hydrogen, lumbered into the sky on the wet and miserable evening of 4 October 1930 to embark on its final, fateful journey. Aboard were forty-two crew and twelve passengers, among the latter being Lord Thomson, His Majesty's noble Air Minister, and apparently a stubborn fool.

The soon-to-be-infamous Lord Thomson was the man responsible for the R101. So fanatical was he about his aerial dream that he adopted the name of the nationalized aircraft factory as part of his title. It was therefore 'Lord Thomson of Cardington' who oversaw the building of the airship at Cardington, near Bedford, and so arrogant was he that, despite warnings galore about the desperately unsafe state of the R101, he stolidly pushed his pet project to its perilous conclusion when, in the most unnecessary disaster in the history of flying, it ended its brief existence as a blazing inferno on a French hillside.

The floating disaster that was the R101 had been long in the making. In 1923 Britain's Conservative government was urged by the Vickers aircraft and engineering firm that giant airships be used for passenger services linking all major parts of the

The R101, the largest flying machine in the world, at her mast at Cardington, Bedfordshire.

The hangars at Cardington, vast enough to house the leviathans of air travel.

British Empire. The government would commission them and Vickers, the nation's most experienced builders of airships, would, of course, be paid to construct them.

Vickers, greedy for the contract, were horrified when the Conservative government fell before a decision could be made, and in 1924 the first Labour government came to power on promises of nationalization and state control. New Prime Minister Ramsay MacDonald and his advisers then made the most astonishing decision. They decided to commission not one but two airships to exactly the same specification: the R100, a 'capitalist' airship, and the R101, a 'socialist' airship. The R100 was to be built by Vickers and the R101 built by the Air Ministry. By some extraordinary set of rules, the government would then decide which of the two would win its accolades and its orders.

No one was more astonished by this than one of Vickers senior engineers, Nevil Shute Norway, now better known as the novelist Nevil Shute. He wrote: 'The controversy between capitalism and state enterprise had

Lord Thomson of Cardington, whose stubborn vanity caused disaster.

been argued, tested and fought in many ways but the airship venture in Britain was the most curious of them all.'

The first problem facing the R101 design teams was the ministry's decision that petrol engines would be unsafe for their airship, choosing diesel engines instead. The Cardington team argued fiercely against this but was overruled. As a consequence, eight-cylinder diesel units were ordered; engines originally designed for railway locomotives. They weighed twice as much as the R100's petrol-power units, were far less efficient and vibrated alarmingly. Such was the weight of the engines and other equipment built into the R101 that it was not until the airship was first inflated and tested that it was discovered that its lifting power was about half of what was necessary. The team immediately began taking out of the craft all the gadgetry that they had confidently built into it. The end result was disastrous …

The gas valves were so sensitive that they leaked perpetually. The propellers broke when put into reverse, and a heavy backward-facing engine had to be fitted in order that the airship could manoeuvre when docking. The hydrogen bags that would keep it aloft rolled around inside the craft. The airship was unbalanced. It bucked up and down dangerously as soon as it was tethered at its mooring mast. The fins, though beautifully streamlined, tended to cause the craft to stall. The R101's outer casing split time and time again. The craft emerged from its hangar one day with a rip 150ft long in its side. It was repaired but exactly the same thing occurred the following day. The airship ended up being covered with patches.

In an attempt to solve the problems, Air Ministry technicians cut the airship in two, inserted an extra gas tank in the middle, put the craft together again and once again hauled it to its mooring tower. Minutes later, however, the whole skin of the airship began rippling in the wind and a 90ft gash opened along its side. The next step was to begin disposing of every piece of non-essential equipment, so out went all the luxurious touches about which Lord Thomson had previously boasted.

Many similar problems had also been encountered by the Vickers R100 team, led by designer Barnes Wallis who was to become famous in the Second World War for his dam-busting bouncing bomb. However, they were overcome, despite its construction in less than ideal conditions. The R100 was being built in a leaky First World War airship hangar at Howden, Yorkshire, where untrained local labour was being used for much of the manual work. Nevil Shute complained: 'The local women were filthy in appearance and habits, and incredibly foul-mouthed. Promiscuous intercourse was going on merrily in every dark corner.' This may have been one of the reasons the R100 was delayed, allowing the R101 to be completed first at Cardington, where a VIP crowd was invited to watch it being floated out of its hangar.

A few weeks later, on 28 June 1930, the mighty dirigible was flown to Hendon, north London, to take part in an air display and immediately appeared to embark on a sequence of aerial stunts. It twisted and turned, then suddenly dipped its nose and

The R101 rises above its docking tower on an early test flight.

dived spectacularly before pulling up sharply. Moments later the aircraft, already too low for comfort, repeated the manoeuvre and pulled out of its dive just 500ft above the ground. The 100,000-strong crowd applauded, unaware that the dramatic show had been entirely unplanned. In fact, the craft's sweating coxswain had been struggling at the controls to avert disaster. Neither was the public ever told that when the R101 was examined afterwards, more than sixty holes were found in the hydrogen bags. The highly flammable gas was pouring out everywhere.

Nevil Shute (*left*) and Barnes Wallis (*right*) both worked on the rival 'capitalist' R100.

All these problems were brushed aside by Lord Thomson. Despite dissension among the designers, fears by Air Ministry inspectors and the alarm of the Cardington team itself, the great man would not be swayed. Thomson had other reasons for pressing ahead with his personal flight to India. He wanted to make a magnificent impression when the airship arrived at Karachi. His ambition was to become Viceroy of India and he hoped that the spectacle would help him achieve that aim, and he had to fly straight away because he did not want to miss the Imperial Conference to be held in London in mid-October.

Lord Thomson announced: 'The R101 is as safe as a house, at least to the millionth chance.' He issued an official directive: 'I must insist on the programme for the Indian flight being adhered to, as I have made my plans accordingly.' So, re-covered, lightened and lengthened, the airship made its trial flight on 1 October 1930. The craft's oil-cooler having broken down, there was no opportunity for any speed trials, poor-weather tests had not even been embarked on, and the airship had not flown at full power. Neither had the R101 been issued with an Airworthiness Certificate. That was simply solved: the Air Ministry wrote one out for themselves.

(**Above**) The pilot's cabin beneath the belly of the R101 on a test flight from Cardington. (**Below**) The mighty dirigible on a flight over London.

Production of the rival R100 had meanwhile caught up, with the bonus that the private-enterprise sister ship had cost the taxpayer somewhat less than the state-sponsored R101. The Vickers airship lacked the beautiful lines of its sister craft but had one significant advantage: it could actually fly! The Vickers team announced a dramatic transatlantic flight of the R101 to Canada in the summer of 1930, and despite Cardington urging a postponement of both inaugural international flights, Vickers gleefully refused. On 29 July 1930, the R100 set off for Canada, completing the round trip successfully.

Lord Thomson, seeing his pet project as a battle between capitalism and socialism, set the R101's flight date to India for early October, piously warning a conference at his Air Ministry: 'You must not allow my natural impatience or anxiety to influence you in any way.' Few believed his hypocrisy. Nevil Shute wrote later: 'To us, watching helplessly on the sidelines, the decision to fly the R101 to India that autumn of 1930 appeared to be sheer midsummer madness.' He said of Thomson: 'He was the man primarily responsible for the organisation which produced the disaster. Under his control, practically every principle of safety in the air was abandoned.'

Lord Thomson proudly stepped aboard the R101, accompanied by his valet, at 6.30pm on 4 October. Agonizingly slowly, the craft left its mooring mast and headed for London on its route across the English Channel and over France. As the rain lashed down on the 777ft-long airship, the weight of tons of water slowed it and

The R100 over Montreal after making its successful transatlantic flight.

made it even more unstable. It rolled and pitched and was flying dangerously low but those aboard were largely insulated from the hazards ahead.

Inside the vast hull, crewmen went about their business while the passengers settled in for the night. The twin-berth cabins formed the upper deck of a two-floor module sealed off from the roar of the engines and the beating of the weather. On the lower deck was the lounge, 60ft long and more than 30ft wide, with wicker settees, chairs and tables, and potted plants disguising the supporting pillars. Outside the lounge ran promenade decks with panoramic observation windows. Also on the lower deck were the ornate dining room, a smoking room and kitchens.

Crossing the Channel, the watch noticed the surging seas perilously close beneath them. An officer grabbed the controls and brought the airship back to 1,000ft. The R101 crossed the French coast where observers estimated its height at only 300ft. At 2.00am, with the wind increasing, the R101 was over Beauvais, northern France, having travelled only 200 miles in more than seven hours. It was then that the nose of the airship suddenly dipped.

In the control car, the navigator looked at his altimeter and was horrified to see that, although it recorded 1,000ft above sea level, the airship was almost at ground level. The gentle hills around Beauvais were higher than he had thought. The engines were put at half speed and half a ton of water ballast was released from the nose.

Below in Beauvais, several citizens were leaning out of their windows watching the strange airship sail by. It passed over the centre of the town, about 600ft above the ground. It was pitching and rolling. The coxswain wrestled with the controls, but the elevators did not respond. The frail fabric at the nose of the ship had split. The wind was gusting in and the hydrogen was pouring out. Then the nose dipped again.

Peering at the looming earth through the window of the control room, the first officer realized the airship was doomed. He ordered his coxswain to race through the hull to alert everyone that the ship was about to crash. The slumbering passengers and crew heard him screaming over and over: 'We're down lads!' Another valiant crewman remained at his post to pull at the wheel governing the elevators in a bid to make the craft climb. He died at his post but, thanks to his efforts, the R101 touched down lightly.

There was a gush of escaping gas, and then a blinding flash lit the sky. Two further explosions quickly followed and a white-hot inferno engulfed the R101. A poacher sheltering in nearby woods, 56-year-old Alfred Roubaille, witnessed the entire event. 'I heard people in the wreckage crying for help,' he recalled. 'I was a hundred yards away and the heat was awful. I ran as hard as I could away from that place.'

Two crewmen trapped inside the hull thought themselves doomed as they scrabbled to tear through the outer fabric, one even trying to bite an opening in it with his teeth. Then a fiery hole suddenly opened and the two men were flung through it. Another trapped crewman found his gondola door blocked by a girder

The wreckage of the R101 after it ended its flight as a blazing inferno on a French hillside.

French gendarmes and firemen sift through the wreckage, and display the flag that Lord Thomson shamed.

that was dripping with blazing cellulose from the hull, but managed to drag it clear with his bare hands and he hurled himself into wet undergrowth below. The gondola of two other crewmen was also engulfed in flames and they believed themselves lost but miraculously a ballast tank split and the water cascaded onto them, putting out the flames. They were the luckiest to be alive that dreadful night.

Of the fifty-four people who had boarded the airship in England, only six survived. Lord Thomson of Cardington was among the forty-eight who perished.

Chapter Four

End of a Nazi Dream (1937)

The airship *Hindenburg* was to the skies what the *Titanic* was to the seas. She excelled in grandeur and style, and boasted every safety feature of her age. Also like the great ship that was doomed to die on an Atlantic crossing, the *Hindenburg* met her end after crossing the ocean, transformed in seconds from a graceful cigar-shaped floating palace into a burning hell.

Her dreadful demise, coming only seven years after the crash of the British airship the R101, finally rang the death knell for this gracious and glamorous form of air travel.

The story of the *Hindenburg* began in 1935 when the airship, designated LZ 129 but subsequently named after the late Field Marshal von Hindenburg, First World War leader and later president of the Weimar Republic, was completed. The largest and most luxurious dirigible ever made, she was considered a national treasure. To the Führer, Adolf Hitler, she symbolized the rise of the Third Reich and incontrovertible proof of the Aryan supremacy he so often bragged about.

To her builders, Luftschiffbau Zeppelin GmbH (the Zeppelin Company) and her owners Deutsche Zeppelin-Reederei (the German Zeppelin Airline Company), she

Like a giant spider's web, the *Hindenburg* under construction.

Emblazoned with the swastika on her tail fins, the *Hindenburg* in her hangar.

was more than a showpiece of Nazi Germany. She was also the safest means of flight and a statement to the world that the age of the airship was here to stay. The vessel had a proud record to live up to: there had never been a fatality in German civil airship travel, and the safety standards were of the highest. Because of the flammable hydrogen inside the *Hindenburg*'s sixteen huge gas cells, all crew members wore anti-static asbestos-impregnated overalls and shoes soled with hemp. All crew members had to hand in matches and lighters before embarking, as did the passengers. If guests wished to smoke, they were seated in a special pressurized lounge. A steward performed the function of lighting their cigars or cigarettes in another room, sealed off by a double door and out of bounds to passengers.

There were sophisticated insulation devices and warning systems to detect any leakages of gas. The *Hindenburg* could have flown on harmless helium, but the only nation producing sufficient quantities of it in those days was the USA, and they withheld it from Hitler's Germany as the war clouds gathered in case it was used for his military arsenal. Apart from that one drawback, every eventuality had been catered for, or so the designers thought.

The quality of the safety precautions was equalled only by the splendour of the state rooms, the dining room, the lounge and bar, which served the speciality of the ship, the LZ 129 Frosted Cocktail: Berlin gin with a dash of orange juice and lots of crushed ice. There was even a lightweight piano, specially made from aluminium, to entertain the thirty-five passengers. Of course, there were also meals and wines of

(**Above**) The Olympic insignia has been added to her flanks to mark the 1936 Berlin Games as the *Hindenburg* floats at her mooring mast. (**Below**) The *Hindenburg*'s dining room awaits its guests.

unsurpassed excellence, served on blue and gold porcelain by chefs and waiters trained in Europe's finest establishments.

The transatlantic runs of the *Hindenburg* went without a hitch in 1936. Throughout that year, she glided effortlessly from her base at Frankfurt across the Atlantic and back under the expert command of Max Pruss, a seasoned Zeppelin commander.

On 6 May 1937, at the conclusion of her eleventh transatlantic crossing, everything seemed to be going equally smoothly. Despite a buffeting by high winds and afternoon thunderstorms that led to a small detour until the storm abated, she approached the American mainland. The craft passed so low over the Manhattan skyline that her passengers – only thirty-six of the seventy passenger seats were occupied – were able to wave from open windows in her vast silver belly as they came almost face-to-face with news photographers perched atop the Empire State Building.

On the final leg of her journey, the *Hindenburg* neared Lakehurst naval station, New Jersey, to make an early-evening landing ... when the unthinkable happened. Within seconds of the guide-ropes being lowered for landing, flames erupted from the body of the great airship which exploded into a towering inferno above the stunned crowd that had gathered to greet her. From stern to bow, the *Hindenburg*, filled with 198,000 cubic metres of highly flammable hydrogen, was engulfed in fire.

The most graphic testimony to the tragic event was provided by a radio reporter who was broadcasting the landing live to the American nation. His emotional speech has since gone down in history. Herbert Morrison was watching the night sky with studious indifference. The airship was running ten hours late because of the bad weather and Pruss delayed the landing still further because of unfavourable rain, wind

The mighty airship flies over the skyscrapers of Manhattan en route to its New Jersey destination.

and cloud conditions, coupled with poor visibility. Finally Morrison was able to describe the airship's arrival:

It's starting to rain again; it's ... the rain had (uh) slacked up a little bit. The back motors of the ship are just holding it (uh) just enough to keep it from ... It's burst into flames! Get this, Charlie; get this, Charlie! It's fire ... and it's crashing! It's crashing terrible! Oh, my! Get out of the way, please! It's burning and bursting into flames and the ... and it's falling on the mooring mast. And all the folks agree that this is terrible; this is the worst of the worst catastrophes in the world. Oh it's ... [unintelligible] its flames ... Crashing, oh! Four or five hundred feet into the sky and it ... it's a terrific crash, ladies and gentlemen. It's smoke, and it's in flames now; and the frame is crashing to the ground, not quite to the mooring mast. Oh, the humanity! And all the passengers screaming around here. I told you, I – I can't even talk to people, their friends are on there! Ah! It's ... it ... it's a ... ah! I ... I can't talk, ladies and gentlemen. Honest: it's just laying there, mass of smoking wreckage. Ah! And everybody can hardly breathe and talk and the screaming. I ... I ... I'm sorry. Honest: I ... I can hardly breathe. I ... I'm going to step inside, where I cannot see it. Charlie, that's terrible. Ah, ah ... I can't. Listen, folks; I ... I'm gonna have to stop for a minute because I've lost my voice. This is the worst thing I've ever witnessed.

That was how, in a choked voice, the weeping Morrison described the death of the *Hindenburg*. (His words 'Oh, the humanity' have since become a stock phrase for

The following seven images show the *Hindenburg* as it approached its mooring at Lakehurst naval station, New Jersey on 6 May 1937. The explosion erupted in the body of the craft as the waiting crowds watched in horror.

The wreckage of what had been the symbol of Hitler's newly-resurrected Germany. The *Hindenburg* was to the skies what the *Titanic* had been to the seas, but both giant forms of transport were equally and horrifically ill-fated.

whenever someone sees something particularly horrific.) Although accurate reports were difficult to confirm as it took only thirty-seven seconds from the first signs of the disaster to the bow of the craft crashing to the ground, other eye-witnesses recall the belly of the ship glowing red before sheet-flame broke from the tail. The night air was filled with the hissing of the fire as it gorged itself hungrily on the gas-filled ship. Explosions could be heard up to 15 miles away as, one by one, the giant gas-bags exploded.

It was a nightmarish scene as passengers and crewmen jumped from windows and doors while the ship thrashed in her final agony. The smell of burning flesh and the screams of the dying filled the night air. Meanwhile, as pandemonium was erupting all about him, Commander Pruss remained at his controls in the command gondola until the ship hit the ground. Miraculously, he and sixty-one of the other ninety-seven passengers and crew survived. Twenty-two crew and thirteen passengers perished, among them the airship's second-in-command, First Captain Ernst Lehmann who, mortally injured, was found crouching in the glowing rubble, mumbling over and over: 'I don't understand, I don't understand.'

Among the horrors of these grim deaths there were reports of sheer luck that saved some lives. Cabin boy 14-year-old Werner Franz was saved by a soaking from a water tank that burst open. The immediate fire around him was extinguished and he managed to drop through a service chute and escape the fury of the blaze unscathed. He also happened to be the last surviving crew member when he died at the age of 92 on 13 August 2014.

So what had turned the safest means of transportation yet known into a death trap? As reporters and concerned citizens scrambled for answers, an official board of inquiry was set up to probe the disaster and pinpoint the cause of the fire. At first, the commission focused on the possibility of sabotage; not unlikely given the *Hindenburg*'s status as a showpiece of the hated Third Reich. Once that had been ruled out, the commission considered numerous other possible causes, including leaking gas valves, static electricity and engine sparks. However, nothing proved definitive.

Despite the outcry, the file on the *Hindenburg* disaster was closed. It would remain so until eight years later, after the end of the Second World War, when it finally emerged that the Nazis had wielded a strong influence over the official inquiry. In fact, it became known that Hermann Göring, head of the Luftwaffe and once heir apparent to Hitler, had actually ordered the commission not to investigate the possibility of sabotage too thoroughly. The destruction of a Nazi symbol was embarrassment enough. Aryan pride could not take another blow by admitting that a fifth columnist had been responsible.

That possibility was raised again thirty-five years later, when Michael Macdonald Mooney claimed in his book, *The Hindenburg*, that the disaster was no accident but planned destruction by a young anti-Nazi saboteur. He identified the perpetrator as Erich Spehl, a 26-year-old blond, blue-eyed airship rigger from the Black Forest, who perished in the flames. He also alleged that both German and American officials agreed to the cover-up because they did not want to spark 'an international incident'. Although it can never be proved that the *Hindenburg* was sabotaged and that Spehl was the misguided culprit, the one thing that can be stated beyond a doubt is that this tragedy was the end of an era when luxury was prized as greatly as speed.

Immediately after the crash, Germany halted all commercial Zeppelin services. The *Hindenburg*'s sister ship, the LZ 130 or *Graf Zeppelin II*, was allowed to be completed but Hitler's new-found antagonism towards airships soon led to the scrapping of all Zeppelins and ended the airship programme.

Eventually the *Graf Zeppelin II* was used to carry out spying missions against Britain. Interestingly, the *Hindenburg* also became part of the German war effort. The wreckage of the once-proud airship, which had peacefully plied the skies in quiet serenity, was shipped back to Germany and recycled into war planes.

The mystery of the *Hindenburg*'s demise remains to this day, although it is now generally accepted that leaking hydrogen had probably been ignited by an electrostatic discharge caused by the bad weather. The airship had gone up in just thirty-seven seconds but what also died instantly that day was the dream of intercontinental air travel by the beautiful and silent leviathans of the sky. Two years after the disaster, Pan American started operating the first transatlantic passenger service using Boeing 314 airplanes, reducing the cost of air travel as well as journey times and ushering in the real revolution in air travel.

Chapter Five

Nightmare in a Tunnel (1944)

It was a freezing night as Train No. 8017 began its regular Thursday night run between the Italian cities of Naples and Potenza. Every carriage was packed, as usual. This was wartime and many of the 520 passengers aboard were planning to buy up as much fresh produce as they could lay hands on from the farms and markets. Not for nothing was the 8017 nicknamed the 'Black Market Express'.

By 1944 the Allies had already defeated the fascist government of Benito Mussolini but Naples, the third most populous city in Italy, was suffering severe wartime shortages, encouraging an extensive black market trade. Neapolitans survived by travelling into the countryside to buy meat, fruit and vegetables to feed themselves, but also to barter for commodities brought in by the occupying servicemen. Often, to obtain this fresh bounty, they would stow away on freight trains to reach their suppliers in the farming hinterland of southern Italy.

The Allied military government which ran the defeated country knew exactly what was going on. Under-the-counter deals were strictly prohibited but officials turned a blind eye to the black marketeers. If they didn't ply their trade, the million-plus inhabitants of Naples would be pushed close to starvation. The last thing the government needed was unrest on the streets.

On this particular night, 2 March 1944, Train 8017 was heavier than usual. The four coaches, forty-two empty box cars and final 'caboose' manned by a brakeman were being pulled by two steam engines, considered powerful enough for a maximum load of 500 tons. At Naples, however, a large party of medical students embarked together with the equipment they had used on a field exercise near Bari. That pushed the total weight to 511 tons.

Chief engineer Matteo Gigliani, in the lead engine, was not unduly concerned about the overloading, but he knew that it would be a busy night. The track ahead led through the Apennine Mountains where some of the gradients would be steep and the rails ice-coated. Gigliani knew he would have to hit top speed well before these sections to have any chance of climbing them. The stokers would have to keep fires well fuelled.

Victorious US troops drive through the ruined streets of Naples.

At Balvano-Ricigliano station, the last scheduled stop before their destination, Gigliani ordered his fireman, Rosario Barbato, to shovel a huge pile of fuel into the furnaces. 'We'll need it for these upgradients later,' he explained. During those few minutes at Balvano one passenger, olive-oil salesman Domenico Miele, took the opportunity to stretch his legs. A few lungfuls of the icy night air fully woke him and he rummaged through his luggage for a scarf. His decision to step off saved his life. When he took his seat again he noticed that almost all his fellow passengers were asleep.

Miele's next recollection was suffering a fit of coughing soon after the train entered a tunnel. He clambered off, using his scarf as a filter, and tottered down the line with the intention of finding a seat in a less smoky carriage. He made it to the vestibule of the last carriage before collapsing unconscious.

Since leaving Balvano the engines had successfully negotiated two tunnels on moderate gradients. They pulled powerfully along a 75ft viaduct and then entered

The entrance to the 2-mile-long Galleria delle Armi tunnel.

the winding, 2-mile-long Galleria delle Armi tunnel beneath a mountain forest. Here though, on the steep gradient, the engines began to slow. Just before the final car, the caboose, disappeared into the mountain, the train ground to a halt.

In the caboose, brakeman Giuseppe De Venuto thought the drivers must have a signal against them. He had heard no warning signal and therefore assumed that everything was in order. However, when there was no progress after several minutes he lost patience, pulled on his gloves and headed into the tunnel to find out what was going on. The sight that greeted him would haunt him for the rest of his days.

Panicking, De Venuto scrambled back down the track and began half-running, half-crawling towards Balvano-Ricigliano station. He hoped the journey might take an hour, still time to get help for his passengers, but he was hopelessly optimistic. The icy track and the pitch-black tunnels meant it would take twice that time to raise the alarm.

A railway worker at Balvano-Ricigliano station points to the tunnel where more than 500 people died.

Meanwhile, back at Balvano, night duty assistant stationmaster Giuseppe Salonia was settled in his office with a newspaper. Having seen off the 8017, he had over an hour before the next train, No. 8025, steamed in. It was not until 2.30am that he realized the next up-line station, Bella-Muro, had failed to inform him of the 8017's arrival. Impatiently, he called them to remonstrate. The answer he got left the words frozen on his lips. No. 8017 had not arrived. It was nearly two hours late.

Salonia told his colleagues he would hold the 8025 at Balvano and check the line himself with one of its locomotives. Hardly had he clambered aboard this engine when he spotted De Venuto emerging from the nearest tunnel swinging a red lantern. As Salonia reached him he collapsed, begging for help to be directed up the track. Salonia asked him again what was wrong. 'Sono tutti morti!' moaned the distraught brakeman ('They're all dead!').

Yet Salonia had no evidence of an accident. He reasoned that any crash or collision would surely have been heard across the quiet, snow-covered countryside. Perhaps the weeping brakeman had taken leave of his senses. Mystified, Salonia picked the man up in his arms and gently carried him back to Balvano to try to uncover the truth. Once in the warmth of the station, De Venuto calmed down and gave a more lucid account of his ordeal. All the same, his words stretched credulity to the limit. Every passenger dead? How was it possible?

By 4.00am, Salonia had roused police and the local military officials, after which he set off up the track in the borrowed engine from the 8025. When he opened the door of one coach it was like a scene from a horror movie. Some passengers were seated, some sprawled on the floor, some leaning against their neighbour. All of them looked asleep, their faces calm and relaxed. Salonia could tell instantly that they were dead. In the engine cabs, it was the same story. One of the engineers still held his hand on the throttle, his head resting on the window.

Tears streaming down his face, Salonia backed his locomotive onto De Venuto's caboose. Then he towed the ghost train with its coachloads of corpses back to Balvano where stunned police officers began carrying the bodies to a temporary mortuary. The death toll has been put as high as 600 and the official Italian government figure is 517 but a reliable estimate is 516 passengers and 4 railwaymen.

Because witness statements were not immediately taken, there is still confusion over the number of survivors. Apart from the brakeman Giuseppe De Venuto, three other crewmen escaped death: fireman Luigi Ronga, who fell in a daze from the 8017 onto the track, plus fellow brakemen Roberto Masullo and Michele Palo (the latter, rather than De Venuto, being recorded in some accounts as first out of the tunnel). Only a handful of passengers survived. One of them was Domenico Miele, initially taken for dead by police but later recovered sufficiently to give his

The horrific scenes as bodies were recovered from the tunnel.

The dead are loaded onto a truck at Balvano-Ricigliano station.

account of what happened. Another passenger appeared so badly brain-damaged that he had no idea who or where he was, or even that his wife and 8-year-old son were among the dead. At least three other survivors slipped quietly away, perhaps concerned that their Black Market activities could come under scrutiny.

So what had happened to the doomed night train? From the survivors' accounts, State police concluded that No. 8017 could not have penetrated far into the Galleria delle Armi tunnel before its wheels began to slide on the icy gradient. The engineer Gigliani could have reversed out and onto the viaduct. Instead he ordered his crew to re-stoke the fires in an attempt to marshal enough power to climb the incline. He and his colleagues on the footplate sweated and strained to do their bit. It was all to no avail. The wheels slid faster but they could not grip.

None of the men toiling in the flickering light of the furnaces could have realized that they were signing their own death warrants. Along with all the other wartime shortages the nation was facing, the railway companies were also experiencing shortages of good-quality coal. The burning of low-grade substitutes produced a large volume of carbon monoxide which is an odourless, poisonous gas. This was a critical factor in the disaster. In the confined space of the tunnel, the deadly carbon monoxide fumes enveloped first the two locomotives and then slowly seeped back to gas the passengers. No one ever suspected danger. Most were asleep and the few who did stir registered only that the train had stopped in pitch blackness.

The tragic story was never properly told until after the war ended. Censorship restricted information to a short official report about the sad 'mishap' that had befallen Train 8017. However, the influential national newspaper *Corriere della Sera*, reporting on 23 March 1944, attributed the catastrophe mainly to:

> A combination of material causes, such as dense fog, atmospheric haze, complete lack of wind, which did not keep the natural ventilation of the tunnel, wet rails, etc., causes that unfortunately occurred all at once and in rapid succession. The train stopped, it slid on the rails and the staff of the machines had been overwhelmed by the produced gas before they could act to move the train out of the tunnel. Due to the presence of carbon monoxide, extraordinarily poisonous, it produced the asphyxiation of stowaways. The action of this gas is so rapid that the tragedy occurred before any aid could be brought from the outside.

Due to the high number of corpses and lack of resources, victims were buried without a religious service at the Balvano cemetery, inside four common graves. Railway employees were the only ones who received a regular funeral service. Neither was there any substantial compensation or redress for the families of the dead. The military government deemed it a 'wartime accident'. As such, it washed its hands of all responsibility.

It was not until 2017 that a commemorative stone was laid at Balvano in a ceremony which was attended by relatives of the victims, along with mayors from the region and politicians. The Italian historian Gianluca Barneschi, who found classified documents about the catastrophe at The National Archives in Kew, London, said at the time:

> It was the first time that national authorities in Italy recognised the disaster. It was the *Titanic* of train disasters, but unlike the *Titanic* it is barely known. It was covered up by both the Allies and the Italians. For the Allies it was a potential public relations disaster: people whom they had liberated died on a freight train in a desperate bid to get food to feed their families. The Allies were accused of

8017

In memoria di coloro che persero la vita il 3 marzo 1944, a bordo del Treno 8017, l'Amministrazione Comunale di Balvano ed i cittadini vollero porre termine all'oblio, affinchè il ricordo perenne costituisca risarcimento morale per le sofferenze di tutti.

BALVANO , 3 marzo 2017

It is only in recent times that plaques have been erected in local municipalities to commemorate what the Italians regard as the largely forgotten 'Titanic of rail disasters'.

censoring the story because it was an embarrassment and they were fearful of the impact it would have on civilian morale. In turn, the Italians tried to pass off responsibility to the British and Americans. When it happened, the Italian authorities claimed that all the people who died were smugglers and boot-leggers and that none of them had bought tickets. It was all part of the propaganda and it was very unfair, because most of them had, in fact, paid their fare.

Chapter Six

Child Victims of Aberfan (1966)

It had been a damp and dismal autumn in the Welsh Valleys. The grey clouds rolled in to saturate the earth and, with 6½in of rain falling within the first three weeks, the fields were turned into mud-baths and the mountain roads became fast-flowing streams. The morning of 21 October 1966 began no differently. A low mist was accompanied by intermittent drizzle. In the coal-mining village of Aberfan, the early risers turned up their coat collars in preparation for yet another dank day, except they were unaware that this day would become very different. A black, slimy, suffocating monster would descend from the hills to destroy the heart of Aberfan by claiming its most precious assets: its children.

At 7.30am, high above the village a giant colliery slag heap, known to the National Coal Board as Tip No. 7, began to shift. Imperceptibly at first, just a few trickles of slurry slipped down the hillside, then steadily gathered pace, lubricated by the rains, the water springs running under the tip and the oily, greasy mud beneath its 100,000-ton mass. Soon nothing would stand in its relentless path.

At 9.15am, the slurry took with it two farm cottages, killing their occupants, before sweeping across a canal and railway embankment and entering Aberfan. In its path was Pantglas Junior School. It was the last day before half-term, with school supposedly ending at midday.

At 9.25am the avalanche engulfed the school and the row of cottages that stood alongside. Eye-witnesses later recalled the terrible grinding and screeching of breaking rocks and wood, of splintering glass, and of the first awful screams of the victims inside, then the silence. One resident recalled: 'In that silence, you couldn't hear a bird or a child.'

One of those witnesses was the Reverend Kenneth Hayes. He rushed around the corner of a village street to see a huge wall of slurry which was rising over the school, moulding itself around the building until it was all but buried. He ran forward in disbelief, responding to a futile impulse to stop the mud-slide with his bare hands. His

(**Above**) The coal slag heap looms over the Welsh mining village of Aberfan. (**Below**) View of Aberfan in a photograph taken from the upper slopes of the slag heap.

The chair is the table.

A class of smiling innocents at the Pantglas Junior School, Aberfan.

9-year-old son Dyfrig was one of the children inside the school. The Reverend Hayes, who would later identify the boy's body as it lay in a makeshift mortuary at Bethania Chapel, said:

> The slurry just overwhelmed the school. I saw the last of the living being taken out and the first of the dead. I knew I had lost my boy, although his body was not found until the following day. That was when the enormity of it all dawned on us. Whole families had been wiped out. I buried five from one house.

Inside the school, the difference between life and death depended on which class-room the staff and pupils were using. Those whose classroom faced the slag heap bore the brunt of its unstoppable destructive force. Those slightly further away had a few precious seconds of warning that gave them time to avoid the inevitability of suffocation.

One of the fortunate ones was 8-year-old Pat Lewis. She stared aghast at the wall splitting open behind her teacher as he called the register. Then she screamed and the warning was enough to get Pat and most of her class outside to safety. Her older sister Sharon was not so lucky. A terrified Pat ran back home where she fell into the arms of her mother, Sheila. Her first words were a mumbling apology: 'I've left my coat in school mam, sorry.' Then the tears poured out as she told what had happened. Grimly, her mother, a trained nurse, swept Pat into her arms and ran to

Aerial photographs taken from different angles showing the vast trail of slurry engulfing the village.

the school. There, climbing through a broken window, she saw a piteous sight. As she described it:

> Inside were about twenty children who had been swept forward by the tip as it bulldozed the building. They were the ones who could be helped, though one of those children walked out of the ruins, seemingly all right, then collapsed and died. I laid the survivors on blankets in the school yard and turned the infants' classroom into a first aid post. I worked the whole day but nobody came out alive after 11.00am. It was the most horrifying day, but your senses sharpen at times like that and so I can remember it all clearly. I knew I couldn't go and identify Sharon's body. My poor husband had to go and do it. He came back from the chapel at about 5.00am on Saturday and said he recognised her. She had been found with the rest of the class and the teacher. I was sitting on a stool by the fire and I remember I slid back against the wall and made a terrible noise for I don't know how long.

Suffocation was the cause of many of the fatalities but fate had played another cruel card. The avalanche ruptured two water mains that supplied the whole of the Welsh

A house is half-submerged by the flow of slurry.

(**Above**) Locals, many of them miners, raced to the school to dig for the children buried inside. (**Below**) A policeman carries to safety a child freed from the school building.

capital, Cardiff. Thousands of gallons flooded into the already saturated slurry and any children still trapped but alive were in danger of drowning.

Families who were first on the scene formed human chains to remove debris. They were soon joined by miners from the local colliery who coordinated a more organized rescue effort. Also racing to the scene were members of the Coal Board mine rescue team. One of them, Len Haggett, said: 'Nothing could have prepared me for the sight of a 20ft to 30ft wall of slurry blocking the road.' Len went inside the broken buildings where almost all the children were already dead but found one 9-year-old boy still breathing. With the water level rapidly rising, he cradled the lad's head to prevent him drowning while, with a superhuman effort, he and fellow rescuers managed to lift a collapsed wall from his body. Fifty years later, for a TV documentary by award-winning film-maker Steve Humphries, Len recalled:

> The water was coming in and around this young lad and we had to hold his head up and back. How we lifted that wall off him that day I don't know but we did, just long enough to get our arms under his shoulders and he came out. That was a moment of pure elation. And if he hadn't have come out, within a few minutes he'd have drowned.

That boy was 9-year-old Philip Thomas who had just walked from the school with a classmate to perform an errand for his teacher. When the mudslide swept into the village he was swept along by it and buried under the rubble. His clearest memory is the pain of the rocks sandwiching his hands, as he recalled half a century later:

> I was buried immediately and when I awoke it was pitch black and couldn't see a thing. I began crying for my mother. Then all I remember was men digging me out and muddy water was pouring, pouring all over me. My right hand was crushed so badly I lost three fingers. My leg was injured, my pelvis fractured, my hair gone. I had bleeding internally and externally and they said I would have bled to death if the mud hadn't caked on me, forming a skin. The force of the mud was such that it smashed my spleen, which had to be removed, and ripped off an ear, which had to be sewn back on. But I was lucky: Robert, the other boy on the errand, was found two days later, dead.

Another survivor due to a twist of fate was 5-year-old Elizabeth Jones, who had been allowed to leave her desk to take some dinner money along to the school secretary's office. She said:

> I only remember being engulfed in masonry and sludge. I was trapped in the school corridor for a long time with the body of a little boy beneath me and by the side of me. When they pulled me out I was still holding my shilling dinner money. I am sure that saved me and I still keep it as a lucky coin. Most of my

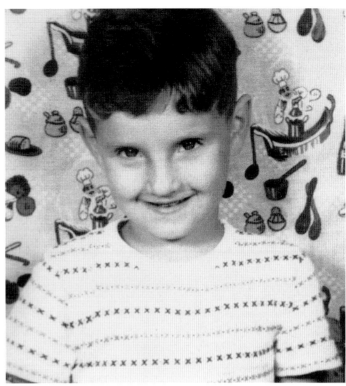

The rescuer and the rescued: Len Haggett and young Philip Thomas.

memories have mercifully faded, when your mind luckily begins to think of other things. But I received severe internal injuries in the slide and as a result will never be able to have children.

Other survivors told how their teacher saw the looming black mountain rearing above the school as he glanced out of the window. Desperately they were ordered to hide under their desks, a move that undoubtedly helped to save some. The little ones thought their teacher had gone mad to be playing such games in class. There were many other acts of bravery that day. Nansi Williams, the school meals clerk, managed to save the life of five children by shielding them with her body but her own life was lost; she was found still clutching a pound note she had collected as lunch money. The deputy headmaster, Dai Benyon, died along with five children as he tried to protect them using a blackboard as a barrier.

Within minutes of the disaster, the whole of Aberfan was descending on the devastated school and its pitiful occupants. Professional rescuers – the fire, police and ambulance services – found scores of willing hands to help them dig. Whether they were doctors or dustbinmen, teenagers or pensioners, the appalling scenes unfolding before their eyes united them in grief and bestowed hidden strengths on them.

Off-duty miners, the sweat on their rock-hard muscles glistening like the tears in their eyes, tore into the slurry with a controlled madness. Perhaps they, more than

Hopes fade as body after body is dug out of the wrecked schoolrooms.

Rescuers reach one of the farm cottages that were first hit by the slurry further up the mountain.

any others present, saw the terrible irony of what had happened. It was they who had toiled beneath the ground to produce coal and dump the unwanted slag. Now the industry that was their life and helped them to raise families had robbed them of their children, many of whom were now being uncovered, still entombed at their school desks.

Throughout the rest of the day the rescue teams worked, calling for silence every so often in the hope of hearing a muffled cry. Darkness fell but the labour continued under the glare of powerful sodium lights. One by one, exhausted fathers were gently led away to their beds for a night in which sleep could never come. Everyone spoke openly of their grief and of cruelly dashed hopes. Mineworker Bryn Carpenter, who had been recovering in hospital after a pit accident, was brought to the school seeking news of his 10-year-old boy Desmond. He said:

> When they told us of an unidentified 10-year-old in hospital our spirits lifted, but it turned out to be someone else. Later that night they found Desmond's body.

We were by no means alone in our grief. In my street alone we lost fourteen. Two houses lost two children each. And time doesn't heal: there is always something there to trigger grief again.

No survivors were found after 11.00am on that dreadful day and it was not until a week later that all the victims were recovered. The final death toll was 144, of whom 116 were schoolchildren, mostly between 7 and 10 years old and 109 of them from the school. Five of the adults who died were their teachers. Most were buried on a hillside above the Bryntaf Cemetery, around a giant cross of flowers laid out by mourners. Their headstones are formed of white arches along two 80ft trenches.

In 1967 a five-month official inquiry, involving 136 witnesses, concluded that the Aberfan disaster need never have happened. Worse, the industry had received warnings from mining engineers that the Aberfan Tip No. 7 was unstable and unpredictable. For six years those warnings had gone unheeded. The National Coal Board was squarely blamed for having no clear policy for safety standards at its slag heaps, and the inquiry report accused its officials

> … not of wickedness but of ignorance, ineptitude and a failure in communications. Ignorance on the part of those charged at all levels with the siting, control and daily management of tips; bungling ineptitude on the part of those who had the duty of supervising and directing them; and failure on the part of those having knowledge of the factors which affect tip safety to communicate that knowledge and to see that it was applied.

White arches surmount the headstones of the dead.

MEMORIAL GARDEN
DEDICATED TO 116 CHILDREN AND 28 ADULTS
WHO LOST THEIR LIVES OCTOBER 21st 1966
TO THOSE WE LOVE
AND MISS SO VERY MUCH
I'R RHAI A GARWN
AC Y GALARWN O'U COLLI.

Plaque in the memorial garden that was laid out on the site of the school itself.

Yet despite blame being apportioned, there were no prosecutions. The tips above Aberfan were eventually removed but only after a bitter campaign by the community. A memorial garden was laid out on the site of the school itself. It is lovingly maintained as a place of peace for the survivors of Aberfan, many of whom still suffer nightmares of being buried alive alongside their dead school friends or suffer feelings of guilt. As one surviving pupil said: 'We didn't go out to play for a long time because those who'd lost their own children couldn't bear to see us. We all knew what they were feeling and we felt guilty about being alive.'

Chapter Seven

Price of the Space Race (1960s)

It was supposed to be a voyage of discovery for mankind. In fact, the 'space race' of the 1960s was as much to do with superpower prestige as it was scientific progress. From the moment on 12 April 1961 that the Soviet Union succeeded in making Yuri Gagarin the first man in space, the US and USSR were plunged into a new facet of the Cold War. Both nations wanted to show the world that their technology was the best. The problem for Washington was the fact that the Soviets had made all the running.

The announcement by President John F. Kennedy on 25 May 1961 that America would put a man on the moon by the end of the decade changed all that. Almost overnight, the National Aeronautics and Space Administration (NASA) found itself with an open cheque book. The *Apollo* space programme was born, dedicated to mankind's first moon-shot, and during the mid-1960s film footage of yet another NASA craft blasting off from Florida's Kennedy Space Center became a familiar feature of worldwide TV news bulletins.

It was not until 1967 that the first *Apollo* rockets were ready. Up until now, spaceships were the safest form of travel known. Dozens of US astronauts and Soviet cosmonauts had gone into Earth orbit, conducted space walks and carried out gravity-free experiments. Each time they returned to Earth safely, their capsules strung beneath nylon parachutes.

Occasionally a note of caution was sounded. Major Ed White, the first American to walk in space, told newsmen on his return: 'As we fly more and more spacecraft we are going to have one come down and probably going to lose somebody. But I wouldn't want that to hold up the space programme.' His words were to prove prophetic.

To the watching public, meanwhile, it all seemed as easy as catching a holiday flight. Unlike the scientists and officials at NASA, people could not easily comprehend the awesome power that was needed to escape the pull of Earth's gravity. Besides, they had a touching faith in American technology. The law of probability, which held that soon something would go wrong, was strictly for doom and gloom merchants.

(**Left**) Yuri Gagarin, the first man in space. (**Right**) In May 1961 President John F. Kennedy announced that America would put a man on the moon by the end of the decade.

Yet not even the most pessimistic space pundit could have predicted how the run of success would end. Kennedy's dream, borne so proudly by *Apollo 1*, was cruelly shattered before the rocket even left the ground. The first disaster in the history of space exploration was caused by nothing more complicated than a loose wire.

For years NASA had been pondering how best to save weight aboard its rockets, thereby making the task of the launch engines easier. One way was to use an atmosphere of pure oxygen inside the capsule. Oxygen makes up one-fifth of our air, the remainder being mostly unbreathable nitrogen. This atmospheric mixture was used in Soviet spacecraft, even though it meant bolting in heavy, cumbersome nitrogen and oxygen cylinders along with equipment to mix the two gases safely. The Soviets had little need to worry about the weight factor. Their giant Proton booster rockets were easily capable of producing the required thrust. They feared that oxygen alone was too combustible.

NASA acknowledged that its *Apollo* rockets were less powerful but claimed the use of pure oxygen would significantly ease their payload. As to the fire danger, scientists at the Manned Spacecraft Center in Houston, Texas, came up with some reassuring arguments. The reason fire spreads, they observed, was because oxygen heated by a flame rises up pulling in fresh, cold oxygen behind it. This intake feeds the blaze and so assists it to expand. However, in space, the Houston team argued, there was no gravity and no up or down. Even if oxygen did ignite, it could not rise in the heat. It would simply smother itself.

Others were not so confident. Two years before *Apollo 1* was due to blast off, NASA's senior medical adviser, Dr William Randolph Lovelace, specifically warned the agency about 'the potential dangers of 100 per cent oxygen atmosphere'. He told how in one experiment, involving a space capsule carried inside an aeroplane at

33,000ft, the tube in a television monitor overheated and dripped molten plastic onto a control panel. The crew smelled the fumes and were able to extinguish the fire. Dr Lovelace argued: 'Instead of focusing attention on the hazards of fire, this accident gave a false sense of security.' He also drew attention to a blaze inside a capsule simulator at the Brooks Air Force Base, Texas. Two crew members in full space suits noticed a dull glow behind an instrument console. Within seconds the console was in flames.

The most serious fire of all was recorded at Philadelphia's Naval Air Center inside an oxygen chamber pressurized to within only a third of the levels planned for *Apollo*. One of four crewmen working in the chamber caused a minute spark as he tried to change an electric light bulb. A flash fire instantly erupted, setting fire to the men's clothes and inflicting appalling burns on them.

NASA could not say it was never warned. Yet by 1967 the project was already too far advanced to make wholesale changes. If Kennedy's challenge was to be answered, the use of pure oxygen could no longer be the subject of debate. Besides, the Soviets were rumoured to be attempting a moon-shot. In Kennedy's honour (the president having been assassinated in 1963), America had to get in first.

The man chosen to command the *Apollo 1* mission was Gus Grissom, certainly no stranger to danger. The Korean War ace had made two previous space flights, the first of which he was extremely lucky to survive. Grissom's Mercury spacecraft splashed down safely in the Pacific, only for the impact to dislodge his escape hatch. Helpless, he had an agonizing wait in his sinking capsule before NASA divers managed to get him out.

A few weeks before the *Apollo 1* mission, Grissom attended a hearing of the US Congressional Space Committee. With him was fellow senior astronaut John Glenn. Grissom nodded enthusiastically as he heard Glenn's blunt words to the congress-men: 'You may as well realize now that some future space flight will fail, probably with the loss of life. There will be failures, there will be sacrifices, there will be times when we are not riding on such a crest of happiness as we are now.'

On 27 January 1967 Grissom, aged 40, reported to Launch Pad 34 at the Kennedy Space Center. With him were fellow crew members Roger Chaffee, 31, a naval lieu-tenant commander eager to begin his debut mission, and the veteran space-walker Ed White, 36. Although *Apollo 1*'s launch date was still a month away, the three had to practise and hone their cockpit drill. That meant strapping themselves into the command module for five-hour stretches at a time, lying uncomfortably on their backs in full space suits. Time and again the men would run through the drill, Grissom giving standard, clipped responses to ground control's requests for the information displayed by his on-board computer.

Like the astronauts, NASA technicians manning ground control's vast bank of monitors found the practice runs rather tedious. The format rarely changed. There

Astronauts (*left to right*) Gus Grissom, Ed White and Roger Chaffee at Kennedy Space Center during training for *Apollo 1* in January 1967.

TV CAMERA ATTACH

The three astronauts in a simulator preparing for what was to be the first manned *Apollo* flight.

was little to do except watch and wait. Suddenly one technician saw his TV screen flash white and then darken. Irritated, he leaned forward to twiddle the brightness and contrast controls. Somehow his link to a camera inside the capsule had been broken. A split second later an agonized yell sounded over the intercom link: 'Fire … I smell fire!' There were three seconds of silence before Ed White's desperate voice confirmed: 'Fire in the cockpit …'. Then came the dreadful sound of the doomed astronauts pounding and clawing at the escape hatch. Seven seconds later Roger Chaffee screamed: 'We're on fire. Get us outta here.' Then silence.

It took four minutes for a rescue team to get from their blast-proof base to the top of the 218ft launch tower. Sprinting out of the high-speed elevator, two of them grabbed *Apollo 1*'s escape hatch handles, ignoring the heat that seared through their gloves. It was already too late. All three men had died in seconds. Although badly burned, autopsy reports confirmed their deaths from cardiac arrest caused by high concentrations of carbon monoxide.

As flames roared out of the command module, the rescue team was forced back. All power to the spacecraft was cut and launch director Dr Kurt Debus ordered the men on the tower to 'Stay away from the capsule. There is nothing you can do for them now.'

For six despairing hours, the bodies stayed in place, clearly visible on the ground-control monitors. Many of the technicians cried openly. Few could bear to look at their dead colleagues. Eventually Debus, who had learned his trade as a Nazi V-2 rocket engineer, decided the danger of an explosion had passed and permitted rescuers to recover the corpses. At midnight they were gently carried out of the scorched cockpit.

Later investigations pinpointed the cause of the fire as a loose wire behind the control panel. Had the capsule's atmosphere been an oxygen-nitrogen mix, it would almost certainly have extinguished itself. In pure oxygen, it sparked certain death.

NASA, however, refused to change tack. The *Apollo* programme was set back eighteen months while spark-proof electrical circuitry was fitted along with a quick-release space hatch. A year after these refinements, on 20 July 1969, *Apollo 11* put Neil Armstrong's lunar module on the moon and Kennedy's dream was fulfilled.

Once America had won the race to the moon, the Soviets decided to counter with another 'first'. On 19 April 1971 they put the world's first permanent space station, *Salyut 1*, into orbit. Then, on 7 June, cosmonauts aboard the *Soyuz 11* rocket managed to dock safely with the *Salyut* and crawled inside to begin what would be a record spell in space of twenty-three days. The three cosmonauts, commander Georgi Dobrovolski, test engineer Viktor Patsayev and flight engineer Vladislav Volkov, completed a flawless mission.

One of the most interesting aspects as far as ground-based Soviet scientists were concerned was establishing how well their bodies would cope with the effects of

Apollo 1 being disassembled following the fire that killed the crew.

The burned-out interior of *Apollo 1*.

On 20 July 1969 President Kennedy's dream was fulfilled: *Apollo 11* put Neil Armstrong's lunar module on the moon.

weightlessness. In zero gravity their muscles would be sapped of strength and tend to go flabby. As the three men began their slow descent home, excited ground controllers reminded them not to try to leave their capsule on landing. Once they were safely on the ground they would have to be carried out by medical teams. Dobrovolski laughed at this. 'Don't worry, we will just sit back and let you do all the work,' he replied.

The cosmonauts of *Soyuz 11* (*left to right*): Georgi Dobrovolski, Vladislav Volkov and Viktor Patsayev.

Illustration showing the flawless docking of *Soyuz 11* with the *Salyut 1* space station.

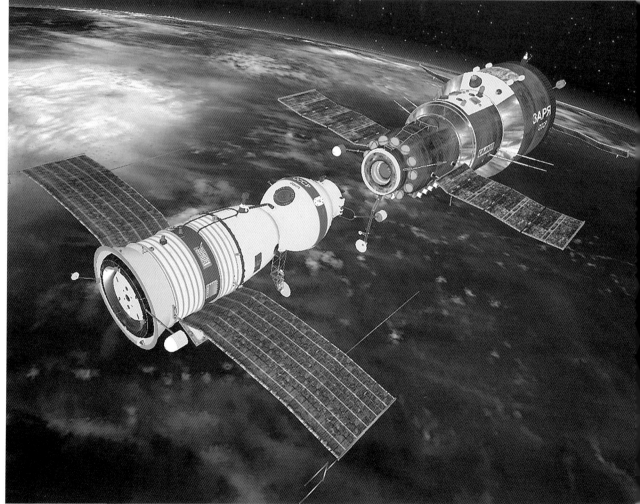

At 23,000ft *Soyuz 11* released its parachutes to begin the gentle glide to Earth. As usual, radio contact had been lost in the scorching heat of re-entry to the Earth's atmosphere. It was never regained. A recovery team was about to find out why. As *Soyuz* fired her retro-engines for a final time to negotiate a perfect landing, medics rushed forward to carry the nation's heroes into helicopters stationed close by. When they opened the main hatch, they witnessed a terrible sight. All three cosmonauts were dead.

It seems that explosive charges used to disengage *Soyuz* from *Salyut* had knocked open a valve in the hatch. Throughout its trip home, *Soyuz* had been leaking air into space. By the time Dobrovolski realized what was going on, the huge forces of atmospheric deceleration, combined with his own muscle weakness, meant that he could not raise an arm to close the valve. All three men had to sit and wait for death to come.

Despite the intense rivalry, the political rhetoric and the national pride that became synonymous with the space race, both sides were united in grief at disasters such as *Apollo 1* and *Soyuz 11*.

On 30 July 1971 *Apollo 15* astronauts David Scott and Jim Irwin touched down on the moon with their sophisticated battery-powered car, the Lunar Rover. During one of their excursions they drove to the edge of a massive chasm, the Hadley Rille, below a 1,300ft cliff. There they gently placed a small metal sculpture of a fallen spaceman and a plaque listing the names, in alphabetical order, of the eight astronauts and six cosmonauts who gave their lives during the first ten years of manned space exploration. The plaque made no mention of the men's nationalities.

Photograph taken by the crew of *Apollo 15* of the commemorative plaque they left on the moon.

Chapter Eight

Soccer's Nightmares (1970s–1980s)

One of soccer's most celebrated legends, Bill Shankly who managed Liverpool Football Club in the 1960s and 1970s, summed up the worldwide love affair with the sport in an oft-repeated quote: 'Some people believe football is a matter of life and death … I can assure you it is much, much more important than that.' Tragically, three horrendous stadium disasters in the following decade showed in graphic terms that he was wrong. Watching football had become, quite literally, a matter of life and death.

The thought that a catastrophe could strike at a league football match had never even occurred to most fans in the 1980s. Perhaps a few veterans of the terraces should have recalled the 1971 disaster at Glasgow Rangers' Ibrox Stadium where sixty-six people lost their lives in a crush during a game against their deadliest rivals, Glasgow Celtic.

The tragedy centred on Ibrox's notorious Stairway 13, where several previous incidents had occurred: one in 1961 when two people died in a crowd crush and a further two in 1967 and 1969 when spectators were injured. The disaster of 2 January 1971 was far more devastating. In this case, 1,000 Rangers spectators were leaving the ground before the final whistle, resigned to a defeat as Celtic were winning 1-0. Then, in the last minute, Rangers scored an equalizer.

It was first thought that the chaos that ensued was because, hearing the roar of the excited crowd still inside, those leaving turned to run back into the stands. Another more likely explanation later emerged. It seemed that a child being carried on his father's shoulders fell off, resulting in a massive pile-up on Stairway 13. Most of the deaths were caused by suffocation, with bodies stacked up to 6ft deep. Among the dead were many children, the youngest aged only 9.

Had steps had been taken to rectify the known crowd danger on Stairway 13, this calamity may well have been prevented. However, it did lead to a huge redevelopment of the Ibrox ground, enlarging its capacity to 50,000 and providing it with a UEFA five-star status. It also led to the *Guide to Safety at Sports Grounds* from the findings of Scottish judge Lord Wheatley, who conducted an inquiry into the disaster.

Workmen examine the dangerous stairway at Glasgow's Ibrox Stadium where sixty-six people died in 1971.

These lessons appeared not to have been learned sixteen years later when home supporters flocked to Bradford City's Valley Parade stadium on 11 May 1985, eager to watch the local promotion match against Lincoln City. Fans were in the mood for an early celebration and the gate was higher than usual. The Yorkshire ground had seen better days. Much of it was built of wood and beneath the seats of the main touchline stand years of discarded rubbish lay in huge heaps. It was out of sight, out of mind as far as club officials were concerned. Later, pre-decimal coins were found by rescue workers sifting through the smoke-blackened wreckage. It was perhaps fifteen or twenty years since this hidden part of the ground had seen a broom.

Close to half-time a fan – we shall never know who – dropped either a cigarette end or a match through the floorboards beneath his seat and onto the tinderbox of fuel below. Soon fire started to smoulder, spreading rapidly. Encouraged by windy conditions, a large area of rubbish exploded into flames and dozens of seats were alight. It took only four minutes for the flames to lick upwards, setting fire to the roof before engulfing the whole length of the stand.

For those inside, it was a horrifying scenario. There were no fire extinguishers; they had been taken away to prevent hooligans using them as weapons. There were no

Fans take refuge on the pitch at Bradford City's stadium in 1985 as the wooden stand goes up in flames.

(**Above**) The wooden stand is engulfed in flames, leaving fifty-six dead. (**Below**) All that is left of the burned-out stand, described as a 'tinderbox'.

emergency exits; the doors at the rear of the stand had been bolted to thwart gate-crashers. Screaming fans were burned alive, many from the flaming tarpaulin fabric that dropped from the blazing roof and smothered them in a blanket of fire. Fifty-six people died, including two children. In one case three generations of a family were instantly wiped out: an 11-year-old boy, his father and grandfather. The only survivors were those who managed to scramble onto the pitch. Others managed to break down the bolted doors, but even some of those were burned at the locked turnstiles.

Just eighteen days later, on 29 May 1985, while British football was still mourning the Bradford fire victims, tragedy struck again. This time the setting was the Heysel football stadium in Brussels where Liverpool FC, then one of the world's greatest teams, were due to play Italian league giants Juventus. From the start, this European Cup final seemed dogged by controversy and ill-will. There was obvious tension on the streets beforehand, with the supporters of both sides involved in taunting and running brawls. When the ground opened and police penned a block of Italian fans at the end of the ground reserved for Liverpool, it seemed to be asking for trouble.

Before a ball had been kicked, trouble arrived. Some Liverpool supporters broke out of their own enclosure and raced across a neutral zone hurling bricks and lumps of metal at the Juventus followers. The Italians tried to escape the onslaught by cramming themselves at the bottom of the stand against an unsafe concrete wall, part of which then collapsed. A sea of humanity toppled over it and onto the pitch.

Belgian riot police are called to the Heysel stadium, Brussels, in 1985 where rioting broke out before the kick-off of the European Cup Final between Liverpool and Juventus.

(**Above**) Angry stand-off between Belgian police and Liverpool fans. (**Below**) The wreckage left when a wall collapsed during clashes between rival fans, leaving thirty-nine dead.

Anyone who witnessed those scenes of panic and death were haunted by them for the rest of their lives: incompetent police officers swinging batons as people suffocated, fighting between rival fans on the pitch and, through the mayhem, the screams of the dying. It took three-quarters of an hour for the first medical help to arrive and by the time order was restored the death toll was thirty-nine, thirty-three of whom were Italian. One Briton died, a man who just happened to be in Brussels and decided he'd attend his first football match. Astonishingly, even though this disaster was later described as 'the darkest hour in the history of (European) competitions', amid this scene of carnage the game went ahead with Juventus winning 1-0. European soccer's governing body UEFA later temporarily banned English clubs from its cup competitions.

The final horror in what had become a decade of soccer stadium disasters also proved the most costly in terms of human life. This time, it was Liverpool's turn to taste the tears of tragedy. On 15 April 1989 fans from Liverpool and Nottingham Forest descended on the Yorkshire steel town of Sheffield to watch an FA Cup semi-final game. Sheffield Wednesday's cavernous Hillsborough stadium had been chosen to host the match for two reasons: firstly, it was a neutral ground, and secondly, it was thought to be big enough to accommodate the huge travelling support anticipated from both sides. A capacity gate of 54,000 was a certainty.

Sheffield police had not had long to plan the management of this large crowd but they had plenty of experience in policing league football. The city had two prestigious league clubs, Sheffield Wednesday and Sheffield United, and officers knew the importance of segregating rival fans before and after a game. It was established policy to delay a kick-off only as a last resort. Delay only caused further disruption to the city's residents.

The turnstiles opened soon after midday but it became noticeable that the West Stand, allocated to Liverpool supporters, was slow in filling up. Officers searching for alcohol and offensive weapons at the Leppings Lane entrance found they had plenty of time to question fans. There were no large queues.

By 2.00pm, some senior officers were privately wondering what had happened to Liverpool's supporters. Experience suggested there should have been around 20,000 Liverpool supporters in place, whereas in fact there was little more than half that number. In the West Stand only enclosures Three and Four, which boasted the best views of goal, were filling up. Nottingham Forest's end of the ground was populated as expected.

It occurred to police that thousands of Liverpool fans would be arriving late and determined not to miss a second of their most important match so far in the 1988/89 season. Yet Chief Superintendent David Duckenfield, the senior officer in charge, ruled that it was not necessary to delay kick-off. He clung to the belief that the fans would still get in by 3.00pm.

In fact the sheer volume of cars and coaches making the trek across the Pennines from Merseyside made Duckenfield's assessment optimistic in the extreme. As the minutes ticked by to kick-off, queues outside the Leppings Lane turnstiles grew exponentially, to the point that many hundreds were arriving while only a handful per minute were being admitted. Officers on foot patrol were already too squashed to offer any guidance or control.

By 2.45pm the situation was fast becoming untenable. Seeing the crush in front of them, previously good-humoured fans began to get frustrated. Others deliberately tried to push their way to the front, oblivious to the effects their actions would have on others. That said, the police handling of the crisis was undoubtedly incompetent. Inside the ground, hundreds of supporters continued to try to pack their way into the popular 'Three Pen' and 'Four Pen' enclosures. The resulting logjam meant that fans queuing behind could not get into the other enclosures. Outside there were 5,000 fans angrily demanding the chance to get in.

The senior officer in charge at the Leppings Lane end radioed Duckenfield recommending that exit barriers be swung open to let the fans in en masse, but the chief superintendent could not make an immediate decision. It was not until eight minutes before kick-off that he agreed to open the gates. Within minutes, 2,000 fans were clawing their way through, with or without tickets. The vast majority made straight for the areas deemed to give the best view: Pens Three and Four. They could not know, because they could not see, that down at the front the first victims were already choking and suffocating to death.

The crush on these fans intensified as the teams took the field. Those still conscious screamed and begged police on touchline duty to open emergency exits in the wire security fencing around the pitch. Their pleas went unheeded. Officers thought they were either cheering on their team or trying to wave to the BBC TV cameras that were broadcasting the match live.

One group of supporters managed to open the gate to Pen Three. Police, trained to spot a pitch invasion in the offing, immediately rallied round and closed it. Other Liverpool fans caught climbing the wire were pushed back like prisoners of war ruthlessly subjugated by their camp guards. Some were jammed and immobilized against crush barriers or fencing. Others began to slip beneath the sea of bodies. All this time the steady, murderous shove from behind them continued.

Four minutes into the match, Liverpool's England star Peter Beardsley struck a sweetly-timed shot which cannoned off the Forest crossbar. In the West Stand excited fans lunged forward and the force of the surge snapped a crush barrier that was already fatally weakened. Dozens of fans suddenly disappeared from view. Many had gasped their last breath or, deprived of oxygen for four minutes, suffered irreparable brain damage.

(**Above**) Fans at Sheffield's Hillsborough stadium are hoisted aloft to escape the 1989 crush as fans arrived for a match between Liverpool and Nottingham Forest. (**Below**) Chaos as fans flee onto the pitch at Hillsborough's Leppings Lane end as others, unable to escape, are crushed to death behind the high fences.

At last the police, for so long on their guard against a pitch invasion, saw the hideous truth. The senior officer at the Liverpool end of the ground radioed Duckenfield warning that the match would have to be stopped. He didn't bother to hear the reply. Instead he raced out among the players, grabbed the referee and urged him to lead both teams off. It was five minutes past three. In the West Stand, ninety-six fans were either dead or doomed.

The security fence access to Pens Three and Four was now flung open and police began the grotesque task of trying to disentangle the barely alive from the bodies of the dead. Young constables stared in disbelief at a sight that would traumatize them for years to come: faces coloured deep blue from oxygen deprivation; corpses with eyes open, tongues lolling; unseeing eyes staring. The smell of vomit and faeces infused the air. Policemen who had buttoned up their uniform that morning in preparation to confront soccer thugs suddenly found themselves taking on the duties of front-line medics. In shock and anger, surviving fans began berating the officers, behaviour that served only to heighten the confusion.

Most of Hillsborough's dead were young men in their twenties. Only seven were women and only three were aged 50 or more. Ninety-four died on the day from asphyxiation. The death toll rose further when a 14-year-old boy's life-support machine was switched off and finally reached ninety-six when artificial feeding was withdrawn from a 22-year-old man in a vegetative state almost four years after the disaster.

Nowhere was the tragedy felt more deeply than at Anfield, Liverpool's home ground. Within minutes of the first news reports, Merseysiders began arriving with makeshift bouquets of flowers in memory of the dead. At first these were dropped outside the entrance gates, but as the scale of the tragedy became clear, club officials ordered the turnstiles to be opened. Within hours the goal in front of the famous Kop terrace was covered in blooms, scarves and messages of sympathy. Some fans linked arms and, through their sobs, sang the Liverpool anthem *You'll Never Walk Alone*.

Had Bill Shankly been alive, it would certainly have moved him to tears. Football was his greatest love, yet he would have been first to acknowledge the legacy of Hillsborough. No sport is worth dying for.

What made the tragedy worse for the families of the ninety-six dead was the length of time it took before they saw a measure of justice. An inquiry by Lord Justice Taylor, not completed until 1990, finally concluded that policing on the day had 'broken down' and cited 'the failure of police control' as the main reason for the disaster. The delayed coroner's report then controversially returned verdicts of 'accidental death'. Due to continuing pressure from the Hillsborough Family Support Group, the government in 2009 set up an independent panel to reinvestigate the disaster; three years later it concurred that 'lack of police control' and not the

Tributes of flowers and scarves quickly turned the goal in front of Liverpool's Kop terrace into a shrine. The death toll eventually reached ninety-six.

behaviour of fans had been to blame. The verdict of the original inquest was quashed and a second one ordered. On 26 April 2016 it found the supporters to have been 'unlawfully killed' due to grossly negligent failures by police and ambulance services in fulfilling their duty of care to the supporters. In June 2017 six people, including David Duckenfield, were charged with various offences including manslaughter by gross negligence.

Chapter Nine

Town's Cloud of Death (1976)

The scene in the little northern Italian town of Seveso could have come straight from a 1950s sci-fi movie. One moment it was just another quiet, sultry Saturday afternoon … the next there was mayhem. Families sitting at pavement cafés began choking. Children playing football in the street started screaming with pain. Birds dropped down dead out of the sky. It was for all the world as though a silent, invisible killer had been unleashed.

Only a few men could hazard a guess as to the cause. Shortly after lunch that day, 10 July 1976, weekend workers at a local chemical company heard a loud bang followed by a strange whistling sound. They ran outside to find a chemical reactor spewing a fine white dust cloud from a safety valve. The men on duty quickly opened up water pipes into the reactor, flooding it to prevent further contamination. The process took several minutes, by which time the cloud was floating inexorably through Seveso and other villages of the Po valley, north of Milan, sparing no one within an area of 6 square miles.

The chemical deposited was dioxin, one of the deadliest poisons known to mankind. It is thought that less than 4oz in water supplies would be sufficient to kill everyone in a city the size of London. In the skies above Seveso that summer's day, there was enough concentrated dioxin to wipe out one-third of the entire population of America.

The chemical factory was run by Swiss-based ICMESA, itself part of the multi-national Hoffman-La Roche pharmaceutical company. It manufactured trichloro-phenol for use in domestic cleaners and anti-perspirants. One of the by-products of the process was dioxin gas. Normally, factories such as this are equipped with huge 'dump' tanks which act as a back-up for when gas is released through safety valves. The tanks are equipped to absorb toxic fumes and clean them up for safe release into the atmosphere. However, the 160 employees of ICMESA in Seveso had nothing quite so sophisticated to hand.

It was not difficult to work out what had gone wrong. A chemical process carried out in the reactor the previous day had failed to cool properly and the residual heat

The ICMESA chemical factory that spewed a chemical cocktail into the air over the Italian town of Seveso in 1976.

influenced the reaction that followed. ICMESA's senior management were made aware of what happened but, initially at least, they kept the knowledge to themselves. Perhaps they hoped the dioxin escape would pass off relatively unnoticed. If so, they could not have made a worse misjudgement.

Over the next few days, hundreds of people presented themselves to hospitals suffering from vomiting, headaches and blurred vision. Worse side-effects soon appeared in the form of a painful and unsightly skin disease called chloracne. Others suffered skin rashes and pus-boils, even backache. All told how the air that Saturday afternoon was heavy with the acrid odour of burning plastic.

Doctors were baffled by the phenomenon and were unsure what treatment to use. It seemed that no family among the 17,000 residents of Seveso had been left unscathed, with more casualties coming forward each day.

Livestock and wildlife seemed to have been particularly badly hit. Farmers found herds of cows bleeding from their ears and eyes. Entire chicken roosts were wiped out. Cats and dogs would suddenly keel over in the street, their fly-covered carcasses left stinking in the sun. One man told how he watched three robins hopping around in his garden, then suddenly drop dead. In all, thousands of pets and farm animals died. Crops also started to wither, appearing to have been scorched.

(**Above**) Hundreds of people, including many children, suffered from painful skin rashes and boils. (**Below**) A field littered with dead sheep. Livestock and wildlife were particularly affected by the poison cloud.

As the weeks wore on, the residents of Seveso and other affected neighbouring communities, including Meda, Desio and Cesano Maderno, began to panic because of a lack of information from the authorities. As there had been no obvious disaster, such as a blaze or explosion, the authorities were unsure which way to turn. The media response was also muted. No TV stations or national newspapers had got to grips with the story. ICMESA itself saw no reason to make a statement. On Friday, a full six days after the leak, all that changed. A 2-year-old child was rushed to hospital with her body a putrid mass of boils and blisters. Doctors who were already highly suspicious of ICMESA's role in the tragedy now lost patience and demanded some straight answers. The mayors of both Seveso and the nearby town of Meda made accusations against the company, which offered a bland, non-committal response. Soil samples, they said, were being analysed by scientists in Switzerland. In the meantime, they advised that posters should be put up around town warning the public not to eat locally-grown produce.

That same night, another eighteen children were brought into hospital. With every hour that passed, it seemed the effects of the poison cloud were becoming more prevalent, yet medical staff could not understand why treatment seemed so ineffective. The advice from ICMESA was that patients had probably been exposed to a dose of the skin irritant trichlorophenol or TCP. It is not surprising that the doctors felt their skills were impotent as TCP is roughly 1 million times less toxic than dioxin. As one biochemist put it later: 'It was a bit like prescribing aspirin for a patient complaining of headaches and then discovering he had a brain tumour all along.'

By now the media had cottoned on to what was fast becoming the scandal story of the year. Reporter Bruno Ambrosi, based in nearby Milan, remembered a few snippets from student science lectures and decided to check out the chemical make-up of TCP. Sure enough, he unearthed a vital clue. If TCP was heated above 200 degrees Centigrade it gave off dioxin. Ambrosi then discovered how dioxin could destroy tissue such as the liver and kidneys, how it could mutate chromosomes to induce cancers and how there was a risk to unborn children of being born deformed. One paragraph from an academic paper sprang out at him: 'It is the most potent small-molecule toxin known to man. Its effects dwarf those of arsenic and strychnine.'

Ambrosi's story was published just as the Swiss scientists confirmed that soil around Seveso contained huge quantities of dioxin. They pointed out that it would not disperse in water and could potentially contaminate the landscape for many years. The Italian government responded by declaring a state of emergency.

On 24 July an evacuation began from the worst affected area of Seveso. Once the 200 families had left, squads of police and carabinieri (military police) threw a cordon around their homes reinforced by 6 miles of barbed wire. Then a team dressed in charcoal-lined protective suits moved systematically through the zone, slaughtering

(**Above**) Eventually all the roads leading into the infested area of Seveso were sealed off by the Italian army. (**Below, left**) Scientists in white overalls take soil samples for testing. (**Below, right**) While two soldiers stand guard, a technician wearing protective clothing and a gas mask sprays a car leaving the affected area.

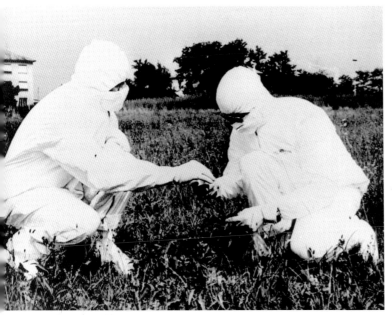

every creature they could find. Most were already close to death. When it was over, more than 60,000 animal corpses lay piled haphazardly in fields and streets. No wonder Seveso was quickly nicknamed the 'Dead Zone'.

The aftermath of the disaster proved to be an unprecedented public health hazard. Thousands of tonnes of soil were removed and encased in concrete. Contaminated plants and carcasses were burned. More than 250 people had to be rehoused. Yet the worst fear of all was the effect that dioxin could have on future generations. Despite frowns of disapproval from some in the Catholic Church, the Italian government declared that abortions throughout the area would be made temporarily legal. At least twenty-six pregnant women who had been exposed to the release had abortions.

Incredibly, not a single person is known to have died as a result of exposure to the toxic cloud and, of the 190 children who suffered from chloracne, all but two made a full recovery.

In 1979 a government inquiry into the Seveso disaster delivered a withering condemnation of ICMESA. It accused factory bosses of using unsafe equipment and expressed disbelief that they had waited twenty-seven hours before informing a low-ranking town hall official of the dioxin danger. Later ICMESA was forced to hand out compensation cheques totalling £8 million.

Five former ICMESA employees were given sentences of two to five years but were freed on appeal or ultimately paroled. On 5 February 1980 the company's production director, Paolo Paoletti, was shot and killed by a left-wing terrorist group.

ICMESA's production director Paolo Paoletti who was shot and killed by an Italian terrorist group.

Chapter Ten

Jumbo Jets Collide (1977)

It was the nightmare of every airline, every pilot, every air traffic controller and of every flying passenger. This ultimate horror, a collision between two giant airliners laden with holidaymakers, happened in the early years of jumbo jet travel but the cause and the blame are still being argued about, and aviation experts now fear that, with our skies and airports becoming ever more crowded, there is a growing danger that it will happen again. What makes this catastrophe even more relevant today is that it was the direct result of a terrorist bomb plot.

The disaster – the worst ever in aviation history, with 583 fatalities – unfolded on the runway of Los Rodeos Airport, Tenerife on 27 March 1977. It was a Sunday, always a busy time on the holiday isle. On this day, however, there was additional chaos, confusion and fear. A terrorist bomb had exploded in the concourse of Las Palmas Airport on the neighbouring Spanish-administered island of Gran Canaria, with the telephoned threat that a second attack was planned. The blast killed no one and the second bomb never materialized. Yet the perpetrators of the attack, a Canary Islands separatist group, never envisaged what carnage their cowardly actions would ultimately cause.

Aircraft heading for Gran Canaria were diverted to Tenerife, which was already encountering handling problems because of thick fog, not unusual for the island where clouds build up around the active volcano of Mount Teide (last eruption in 1909). Among the diverted aircraft were two Boeing 747 jumbo jets: Pan American 'Clipper Victor' flight 1736 from Los Angeles via New York, and Dutch KLM flight 4805, code-named '*Rijn*' (Rhine), from Amsterdam.

As the afternoon wore on, the flight crew of both aircraft received the welcome news that Las Palmas Airport had been cleared for landing. At last they were on their way to their rightful destination. By now, the swirling fog had reduced visibility to less than 500 metres; low but still within the permitted limits for take-off.

Because of the congestion around the airport, both pilots were ordered by the control tower to taxi their respective planes up the main runway to the take-off starting-point at the far end.

(**Above**) The island of Tenerife with Mount Teide in the distance. On 27 March 1977 the cloud around the peak was dense and a thick fog had also descended. (**Below**) Los Rodeos Airport, now known as Tenerife North since a new international airport was built on the south of the island.

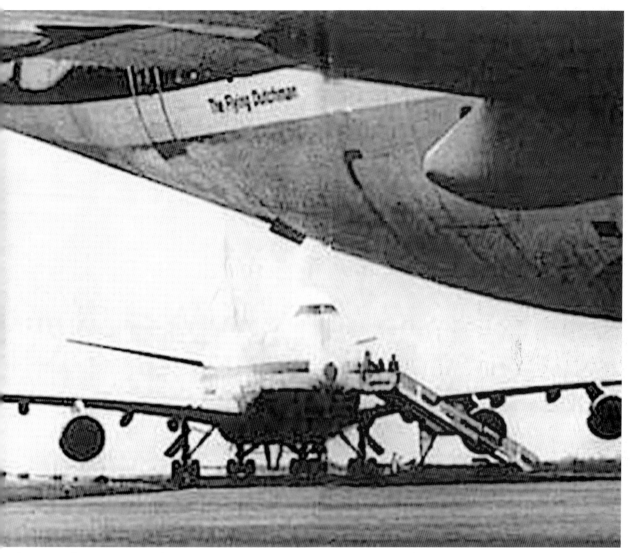
A poor-quality photograph of the two doomed jumbo jets while waiting in the fog at Los Rodeos Airport, Tenerife.

Pan Am pilot Victor Grubbs, an ultra-cautious old stager with an impeccable safety record, breathed a sigh of relief. Soon he and his 380 passengers, mostly vacationers from California on their way to rendezvous with an American cruise ship, would be on their way towards the blue skies beyond the clammy fog bank.

Somewhere out of sight ahead of him, aboard the KLM jumbo, sat his counterpart, Captain Jacob Veldhuyzen van Zanten. He too was peering anxiously through the flight deck windows as he taxied up the main runway ready to perform a circle to reach his take-off position.

Captain van Zanten was also a long-serving pilot. He had been with KLM for twenty-seven years and had appeared in the airline's advertisements to underline their expertise and their safety record. In his supposedly safe hands that day were

KLM pilot Jacob Veldhuyzen van Zanten who had appeared in the company's advertisements as a symbol of the airline's experience and safety record.

234 Dutch passengers who had also been bound for Las Palmas before their flight had been diverted.

From this point, the story of this slow-moving disaster is most graphically told through the voices of those on the flight decks of the two planes and in the control tower, captured on tape (and reproduced here in full).

Captain van Zanten's instructions from the control tower are: 'Flight 4805, taxi straight ahead to the end of the runway and make backtrack.' The jumbo completes this manoeuvre and the co-pilot reports: 'KLM is now ready for take-off and we are waiting for clearance.'

The Pan Am jumbo, meanwhile, had been receiving instructions to taxi up the runway behind the KLM jet, but to turn off by one of the exits on the left, thus leaving the main runway free for KLM to take off. The controllers ask Captain Grubbs whether he has completed his turn-off, and when he replies that he has not yet done so, they instruct him to report to them when the runway is clear.

From this point, a chain of confusing messages passes between the control tower and the two airliners, the recordings of which have been analysed and argued over ever since. Inexplicably, the KLM pilot announces: 'We're going.' The control tower, apparently not understanding, replies: 'OK.' Listening in from the Pan Am flight deck, the co-pilot, First Officer Robert Bragg, exclaims: 'No ... Eh?' The control tower, still addressing the KLM plane, adds: 'Stand by for take-off, I will call you.'

By now, the Pan Am jumbo should have cleared the main runway and turned into one of the taxiways to its left, but it has missed the exit in the fog and is still trundling

The Boeing 747 flown to Tenerife by van Zanten, marked PH-BUF, and a Pan Am 747 of the type that was hit by the KLM airliner.

directly towards the unseen KLM plane. Captain Grubbs and co-pilot Bragg are heard chatting to one another about how 'anxious' the Spanish controllers are to get the planes off the ground, the co-pilot adding: 'Let's get the hell out of here!'

Their frustrated tone is about to turn to one of sheer panic. For, unseen through the thick fog, Captain van Zanten and the invisible KLM jumbo have started moving: straight towards Captain Grubbs and his Pan Am jumbo which is still on the main runway.

Even at this last minute, disaster is almost averted by the intervention of the KLM's third officer, flight engineer Willem Schreuder, who questions his captain's judgement, twice asking: 'Is he not clear then, that Pan Am?' Emphatically, Captain van Zanten answers: 'Oh yes.'

It is just before 5.06pm local time … and the ultimate aviation nightmare suddenly becomes reality. Grubbs can scarcely believe his eyes as the lights of the KLM jet emerge through the fog. His first thoughts are that the mist must be lifting and the jumbo ahead of him is still stationary. Then, as the lights grow brighter and closer, the awful truth dawns … the Dutch aircraft is bearing down on him at take-off speed of 160 miles per hour.

Grubbs yells into his headset: 'There he is! … Look at him! … Goddamn … that son of a bitch is coming!' He shouts: 'Get off! Get off! Get off!'

Van Zanten is by now also aware of the disaster looming. He watches the Pan Am plane slewing round in front of him in a vain attempt to get off the runway and out of his path, but his speed is such that he cannot stop. He has reached the point of no return. The Dutch pilot desperately wrestles with the controls to make the KLM jumbo lift off from the runway early; in effect, hopping over the Pan Am plane in front of him. However, he is too late. The nose lifts but the tail remains on the runway, digging a trench in the tarmac.

Two seconds later, the bottom of KLM 4805 hits the top of Pan Am 1736. The belly of the KLM plane smashes into the forward part of the Pan Am craft's second-class section, while the left wing slices off the roof and bubble of the cockpit. Pan Am 1736 is cut in half. Blazing, it collapses onto the side of the runway.

Aboard the American plane there is confusion. Some passengers fall burning to the ground. The luckier ones pick themselves up and dazedly stumble to safety. Others are too stunned to move and are consumed by the flames where they sit rooted to their seats. The air hisses with death screams.

Meanwhile, the Dutch plane has slammed back onto the runway, skidded round in a circle and come to a halt 300 metres down the runway. There is a moment's stillness. Then it explodes in a fireball, the inferno gorging on itself and on the freshly-filled fuel tanks. Steel and aluminium vaporize.

A total of 583 people lost their lives that Sunday evening in the worst disaster in aviation history. All 234 passengers and 14 crew aboard the KLM plane were killed. Of the 396 passengers and crew of the Pan Am jumbo, only 70 escaped and 9 of them died later in hospital. The final toll was 326 passengers and 9 crew.

The survivors (fifty-six passengers and five crew) included Captain Grubbs, his first officer, his flight engineer and Briton John Cooper, a Pan Am mechanic who was riding the flight deck as a passenger. Mr Cooper, then 53, was thrown out and suffered only minor cuts. He said: 'There was a terrible crash. I just don't want to remember it. There were people screaming terribly: women and children enveloped in flames. I will never get the sounds of that screaming out of my ears.'

Two tragic lies came to light after the crash. Among the dead was a Dutch businessman who had told his wife he was flying to attend a company meeting in Switzerland. Instead he boarded KLM 4805 to spend an illicit holiday with an attractive

Survivors, some lying on the grass, some standing in shock, watch the inferno resulting from the collision of the two jumbo jets.

Pan Am pilot Victor Grubbs watches as fiery explosions engulf his and the KLM aircraft.

woman neighbour. Before setting out, he wrote a card to his wife and gave it to a colleague to post in Zurich. The card, complete with loving greetings, arrived two days after his death. On the same flight was a wife who had told her husband she was going on a Spanish holiday with other girls. Instead she flew off to her death with one of her husband's best friends.

What of the man who set in motion the terrible chain of events on 27 March 1977? Antonio Cubillo was the leader of the Canary Islands separatist movement whose armed wing planted the small bomb in a florist's shop at the larger Las Palmas Airport on Gran Canaria. Cubillo always denied direct responsibility and blamed 'fate'

(**Above**) The burned-out tailplane of the KLM jumbo jet on the runway of Los Rodeos Airport. (**Below**) Landing gear from one of the wrecked airliners.

Transcript of the tape

Tower: 'Clipper 1736 Tenerife.'

Pan Am co-pilot: 'We were instructed to contact you and also to taxi down the runway, is that correct?'

Tower: 'Affirmative, taxi into the runway and leave the runway third, third to your left' [followed by background conversation in the tower].

Pan Am co-pilot: 'Third to the left, OK?'

Pan Am flight engineer: 'Third, he said.'

Pan Am pilot: 'I think he said first.'

Pan Am co-pilot: 'I'll ask him again.'

Tower: 'KLM 4805, how many taxiways did you pass?'

KLM [unknown]: 'I think we just passed Charlie four now.'

Control: 'OK, at the end of the runway make one-eighty and report ready for clearance' [followed by background conversation in the tower].

Pan Am co-pilot: 'The first one is a ninety-degree turn.'

Pan Am pilot: 'Yeah, OK.'

Pan Am co-pilot: 'Must be the third. I'll ask him again … Would you confirm that you want Clipper 1736 to turn left at the third intersection?'

Tower: 'The third one, sir; one, two, three, third, third one.'

Pan Am pilot: 'That's what we need right, the third one?'

Tower: '*Uno, dos, tres.*'

Pan Am pilot: '*Uno, dos, tres.*'

Tower: '*Tres, uh, si.*'

KLM co-pilot: 'KLM 4805 is now ready for take-off and we're waiting for our ATC clearance.'

Tower: 'KLM you are cleared to the Papa Beacon; climb to and maintain flight level nine-zero right turn after take-off.'

KLM co-pilot: 'Ah roger, sir, we're cleared to the Papa Beacon flight level nine-zero … and we're now at take-off.'

KLM pilot: 'We're going.'

Control: 'OK.'

Pan Am co-pilot: 'No … Eh?'

Control: 'Stand by for take-off, I will call you.'

Pan Am co-pilot: 'And we're still taxiing down the runway, the Clipper 1736.'

[Other radio transmissions cause a shrill noise in the KLM cockpit – messages not heard by KLM crew.]

Tower: 'Roger 1736, report when runway clear.'

Pan Am co-pilot: 'OK, we'll report when we're clear.'

Tower: 'Thank you.'

Pan Am pilot: 'Let's get the hell out of here!'

Pan Am co-pilot: 'Yeah, he's anxious isn't he.'

Pan Am flight engineer: 'Yeah, after he held us up for half an hour. Now he's in a rush.'

KLM flight engineer: 'Is he not clear then?'

KLM pilot: 'What do you say?'

KLM flight engineer: 'Is he not clear, that Pan Am?'

KLM pilot: 'Oh yes' [stated emphatically].

[Pan Am pilot sees landing lights of KLM at approximately 700 metres.]

Pan Am pilot: 'There he is … Look at him! Goddam, that son-of-a-bitch is coming! Get off! Get off! Get off!'

[Scream from KLM flight deck and then the sound of collision.]

for the disaster. From his exile in Algiers, he said: 'The Spaniards did not want holiday-makers to see the damage at Las Palmas, so it was their fault that the planes crashed. I do not have 583 deaths on my conscience.'

So who was to blame? The answer is still being debated but, at the time, the verdict depended entirely on which nation was judging the evidence, with fundamental disagreement between the various investigative bodies. Although KLM ultimately admitted responsibility for the accident and agreed compensation for relatives of all the victims, the Dutch investigators initially accused the Americans of being at fault for staying on the runway and not exiting at the earliest turn-off. The Dutch also sensationally accused the Spanish air traffic controllers of listening to a soccer game on the radio. A 'contributing factor', it was agreed, was the so-called 'squelched' radio messages: calls between the planes and the control tower cancelling each other because they were broadcast at precisely the same instant.

There was agreement between both the Spanish and American investigations, however, in pointing the finger at the KLM pilot. Captain van Zanten was said to have begun his take-off roll without permission and to have continued even when the Americans reported they were still on the runway. Van Zanten was also condemned for denying his flight engineer's suggestion that Pan Am was still in their path.

Thus one of the world's most experienced airline pilots, conveniently dead, was landed with most of the blame for the world's worst aviation disaster. It seemed unbelievable. So much so that when the chief executive of KLM first heard about the disaster, his instant reaction was to try to locate his best officer to lead the investigation team: Captain Veldhuyzen van Zanten.

Chapter Eleven

Shattered Dream of Space (1986)

It was the biggest day in Christa McAuliffe's short life. Selected from among more than 11,000 schoolteachers, she had been chosen by NASA to be the first civilian in space. Her brief was to teach two fifteen-minute lessons from the space shuttle *Challenger* as it orbited around the Earth. Across America, millions of children would tune in to her words via closed-circuit television.

On the morning of 28 January 1986 the seven astronauts entered their craft on the launch-pad of Cape Canaveral and began the exhaustive task of checking all systems through the on-board computer. Commander Dick Scobee and pilot Michael Smith were strapped into the front of the flight deck. Behind them sat electrical engineer Judith Resnik and physicist Ronald McNair. Below on the mid-deck were Greg Jarvis, another electrical engineer; Ellison Onizuka, an aerospace expert; and Christa.

NASA's 'ice team' – scientists responsible for spotting ice build-up on the exterior of the shuttle and the booster rockets – had already given the spacecraft a thorough examination. Officials had sent them out three times since dawn, concerned that freezing temperatures the previous night could cause problems. The main worry was that ice might break off during launch and damage *Challenger*'s heat-resistant tiles. No one took much notice of an entry in one of the team's reports noting 'abnormal cold spots' on the right-hand booster rocket.

The on-board computer detected no internal malfunctions. At 'T minus seven minutes and thirty seconds' the walkway was winched back from the launch-pad, leaving the seven astronauts to make their final observations. Below them, 500,000 gallons of liquid oxygen and liquid hydrogen and a million pounds of solid fuel were ready to feed the main engines. The atmosphere in the cockpit was typical of the twenty-four previous shuttle missions: calm efficiency tinged with a hint of tension.

Yet had the seven crew realized that an argument over safety was raging behind the scenes at NASA, it is doubtful that any of them would have stepped aboard. A meeting had been called during the previous evening between NASA officials and engineers from Morton-Thiokol, the makers of the booster rockets. The Thiokol contingent were worried about the cold weather and the effect it would have on the

Challenger's crew: *(from left, front row)* Michael Smith, Dick Scobee, Ronald McNair; *(back row)* Ellison Onizuka, Christa McAuliffe, Greg Jarvis and Judith Resnik.

efficiency of the rubber 'O-rings' used to seal joints in the four segments of the boosters. If the rings became too brittle, they might fail to sit snugly and could allow exhaust gases to escape. Thiokol's team stressed that below temperatures of 10 degrees Centigrade the rings would be less supple. At Cape Canaveral the thermometers had dropped below freezing on the eve of the launch.

The engineers were unanimous. The flight should be delayed, but NASA was having none of it. They had already postponed take-off three times since the original 25 January launch date. First a dust cloud had hit the emergency landing area in Senegal, then rain at Cape Canaveral posed a threat to the heat-resistant tiles. A jammed bolt on an exterior hatch and then strong winds caused more delays. As discussions between NASA and Thiokol grew heated, one of the senior shuttle project officials asked: 'My God, when do you want me to launch? Next April?'

Crew members (*from left*): Smith, Onizuka, Resnik and Scobee during training in a shuttle simulator.

Allan McDonald, director in charge of the engineers, would still not give way. He refused to sign documentation giving official technical approval to the launch. 'I argued before and I argued after,' he later told journalists. Eventually McDonald and his men were overruled when a senior vice president at Morton-Thiokol, Jerald Mason, explained that he had to 'make a management decision'. He and two other vice presidents approved the launch as scheduled.

As countdown continued, crowds massed around the Kennedy Space Center, their cameras at the ready. They knew the aims of the mission included launching a new communications satellite and monitoring Halley's Comet. Now they could follow the final moments before launch with the help of a NASA commentator. As he announced 'T minus forty-five seconds and counting', the excitement grew to fever pitch. Even though this was the twenty-fifth space shuttle mission, it still attracted huge interest among the American public. Besides, many close relatives of the astronauts were present in the VIP section of the public area.

Christa's family was standing with eighteen of her third-grade pupils. They had travelled the 1,500 miles from Concord, New Hampshire, to watch history in the making and, as *Challenger*'s mighty engines roared into life, they craned their necks, desperate to get a good view.

'Four … three … two … one and lift-off. Lift-off of the twenty-fifth space shuttle mission. And it has cleared the tower.' Smoothly and gracefully, *Challenger* rose through the clear blue skies, rolling lazily onto her back as the computer selected a course to exit Earth's atmosphere. At twenty seconds into the flight, Mission Control said that all three engines were running smoothly. At fifty-two seconds, Mission Control instructed: '*Challenger*, go at throttle up.' Scobee replied: 'Roger, go at throttle up.'

Suddenly a dull orange glow emerged between the belly of the shuttle and one of the booster rockets. It was invisible to spectators on the ground but to observant TV viewers, taking advantage of NASA's powerful telescopic cameras, it was unmistakeable. A moment later, *Challenger* was in flames. Seventy-three seconds into the flight, she exploded.

The white plumes of smoke billowing crazily above Cape Canaveral stunned the crowd into silence. Then the scream of one woman was picked up by TV reporters' microphones. Her words were flashed around the world: 'Oh my God! What's happened?'

Seemingly cruelly, the launch commentator carried on as if nothing had happened. 'One minute fifteen seconds,' he droned. 'Velocity 2,900 feet per second. Altitude 9 nautical miles. Down-range distance seven nautical miles.' He was not looking at a TV screen but programmed flight data for what should have been the shuttle's progress. Eventually the unreal monologue was halted. A full minute passed before

Challenger's lift-off for the twenty-fifth space shuttle mission.

Crowds watch the launch open-mouthed as *Challenger* rises into the clear skies over Florida.

the horrified and weeping crowds heard the loudspeakers again crackle to life: 'We have a report from the flight dynamics officer that the vehicle has exploded. The flight director confirms that.'

Minutes later, the news was relayed to Washington. Vice President George Bush and White House Director of Communications Pat Buchanan rushed into the Oval Office where President Ronald Reagan was working. Buchanan knew there was no point in breaking it gently. 'Sir,' he said, 'the shuttle has exploded.' It had been Reagan's idea to make the first civilian in space a schoolteacher and he was devastated. His first question was to ask if any crew member had survived, but the eyes of his aides already told him the awful truth. In fact, NASA would later grudgingly reveal that the crew had survived the initial explosion and were conscious for much of the cockpit's free-fall back to the surface. However, they died instantly when it hit the sea at terminal velocity.

A few hours later, Reagan made one of his most powerful speeches to a nation in shock. Development of the shuttle had convinced most Americans that space travel

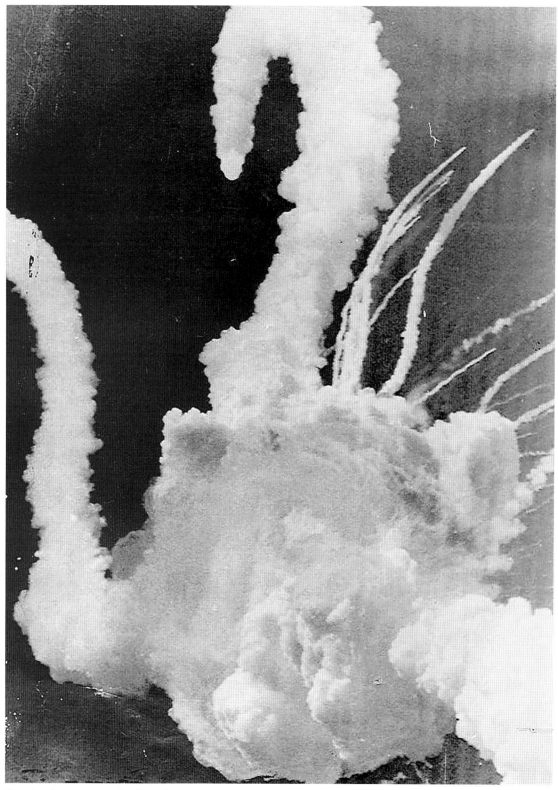

Shortly after commander Dick Scobee sends his last transmission, 'Go at throttle up', *Challenger* explodes.

(**Above**) Disbelief then shock … seventy-three seconds after launch, the crowd's cheers turn to tears. (**Below**) Debris from the space shuttle shoots in different directions. Among the plumes of smoke is the capsule containing the seven crew.

was safe and reliable. More than that, it had become a symbol of their country's standing in the world. Reagan told his audience:

> The crew of the space shuttle *Challenger* honored us by the manner in which they lived their lives. We will never forget them, nor the last time we saw them, this morning, as they prepared for their journey and waved goodbye and slipped the surly bonds of Earth to touch the face of God.

Then, in a poignant address aimed specifically at children, he added: 'I know it's hard to understand that sometimes painful things like this happen. It's all part of the process of exploration and expanding man's horizons.'

None felt it harder than Christa McAuliffe's pupils. For months afterwards they needed counselling for varying degrees of post-traumatic stress disorder. Four days after the accident, Reagan continued his theme at a memorial for the seven dead in front of 6,000 NASA employees, politicians and the bereaved. Turning to the families of the astronauts, he told them:

> The sacrifice of your loved ones has stirred the soul of our nation and, through the pain, our hearts have been opened to a profound truth: the future is not free. Dick, Mike, Judy, El, Ron, Greg and Christa, your families and your country mourn your passing. We bid you goodbye, but we will never forget you.

It was the end of a defining week in Reagan's presidency. So much of his political agenda had rested on the shuttle's success. His dream of a 'star wars' defensive network in which laser-equipped satellites would shoot down Soviet missiles in space relied on NASA to put the hardware in orbit. Suddenly, the agency's ability to perform this task was under question.

In the weeks ahead, the US Coast Guard and NASA recovered amazingly large shuttle fragments from the Atlantic seabed. Despite the power of the explosion, some sections of the shattered fuselage were 25ft long and the cabin containing the bodies was found intact. Each shuttle part was methodically logged to help investigators pinpoint the cause of the tragedy. Of that there was little doubt. At least one of the 0.25in-thick, 37ft-long O-rings had begun to burn soon after take-off, igniting the highly-combustible gases in the right booster rocket. It was the same booster on which NASA's ice team had recorded abnormal cold spots on the morning of the launch. The engineers had been right to worry.

A Senate sub-committee later avoided pinning blame for the disaster on any named individuals but it noted 'a serious flaw in the decision-making process' and submitted a 285-page report calling for a major redesign of key shuttle technology. NASA took note. By the time the next shuttle, *Discovery*, returned to flight a full thirty-two months after the *Challenger* disaster, technicians had made 210 changes to the craft itself and 100 improvements to its computer software.

Chapter Twelve

The Nuclear Nightmare (1986)

A team of Russian physicists arrived at the Chernobyl nuclear power plant in Ukraine, then part of the Soviet Union, in the spring of 1986 to begin a series of tests on an ageing reactor. The work was routine but the men were well aware of the awesome forces they were dealing with. At first, all went well.

The RBMK reactor worked by using uranium fuel rods to boil water and the steam produced was then forced through turbines to produce electricity. Provided there was always enough cold water entering the system, a perfect balance would be maintained. The rods would be kept cool and a steady output of steam would be emitted. As the scientists shut down the reactor to begin their tests, this stability was uppermost in their minds.

Tragically their painstaking calculations proved pointless. All it took to trigger the world's worst nuclear accident was for no one to notice until it was too late that the plant's water circulation system had failed. With no coolant, the uranium rods began to burn themselves – the so-called 'meltdown scenario' – and temperatures at their core touched a staggering 5,000 degrees Fahrenheit. The steam they produced was now radioactive. It reacted with a zirconium alloy, causing it to give off highly explosive hydrogen gas.

In effect, Chernobyl had transformed itself into a nuclear bomb, and what a bomb it proved to be. About 1.5 tons of highly radioactive material was blasted many thousands of feet into the air. The explosion produced ten times as much radiation as the US atomic devices dropped on Hiroshima and Nagasaki in 1945. A poison cloud of radioactivity swept west across Europe as far as the hill farms of Wales and Cumbria in the UK and down the west coast of France. Hundreds of thousands of beef cattle and lambs were declared unfit for consumption. Moscow's reaction? The communist rulers kept quiet.

Yet such was the enormity of the Chernobyl disaster that this was one news item even the Kremlin could not control for long. At 9.00am on 28 April, Swedish technicians at Forsmark nuclear power station, 60 miles outside Stockholm, began picking up bizarre Geiger counter readings on their computer screens. Persistent warning

The Chernobyl nuclear power plant was ripped apart by an explosion in the early hours of 26 April 1986.

As a poisonous radioactive cloud drifted westwards, the initial response of the Soviet authorities was to cover up the scale of the catastrophe.

bleeps told them that a massive radiation leak was taking place. Desperately, the team began checking all their monitoring equipment and gauges in an effort to try to pin it down. It was a fruitless exercise. Forsmark was operating normally, yet every one of its 600 workers had been exposed to radiation levels at least four times above approved safety limits. The Swedish scientists called Stockholm and broke the bad news. The Soviet Union seemed to be the source. It was not until 9.00pm that day that Moscow owned up. A brief item on the evening news reported a statement from the authorities that read: 'An accident has taken place at the Chernobyl power station and one of the reactors was damaged. Measures are being taken to eliminate the consequences of the accident. Those affected by it are being given assistance. A government commission has been set up.'

Scarcely pausing for breath, the newscaster moved on to his next story about a new Soviet peace fund. It was a scandalous way to report the worst accident in thirty-two years of commercial nuclear power, and it revealed nothing of the heroic fire-fighters who, at that very moment, were sacrificing themselves by exposure to radiation. The officer leading the fire teams, Lieutenant Colonel Leonid Telyatnikov, had been on holiday leave but raced to the scene at 1.32am on 26 April, exactly nine minutes after the explosion. He and his twenty-eight men began fighting the flames, protected by nothing more than hard hats and Wellington boots. Chernobyl had begun pumping more than 100 million curies of radiation into the atmosphere and within minutes, the first firefighters had sustained lethal doses. Telyatnikov later described the dramatic rescue operation from the moment he first sighted the crippled reactor:

> I had no idea what had happened or what we were heading into but as I approached the plant I could see debris on fire all around like sparklers. Then I noticed a bluish glow above the wreckage of Reactor 4 and pockets of fire on surrounding buildings. It was absolutely silent.
>
> I realised it was not an ordinary situation as soon as I passed through the gate. There was just the noise of machines and the fire crackling. The firefighters knew what they had to do and proceeded quietly, on the run. The radiation-measuring metres had frozen on their highest level. Thoughts of my family would flash through my mind and be gone. No one would discuss the radiation risk. The most frightening thought was that we wouldn't have enough strength to hold out until reserves came.
>
> About an hour after the fire began a group of fire-fighters with symptoms of radiation exposure were taken down from a rooftop close to the damaged reactor. When I approached five men to take up the position, they rushed to the rooftop almost before I could get the words out of my mouth. They are all dead now from radiation poisoning.

So too is Lieutenant Colonel Telyatnikov himself. Having climbed onto a blazing reactor roof to organize the operation, he did not escape the dreadful effects of the fire. For years after, he was one of the Chernobyl veterans dubbed 'the living dead' by Russians and his life became a constant battle against cancer. He died in Kiev in 2004, aged 53.

Despite the obvious scale of the catastrophe, three days into the disaster the Soviet hierarchy was still playing it down. Moscow at first rejected offers of scientific help from Stockholm, regarding that as unnecessary Western meddling. However, as the extent of the crisis became apparent, they asked West German experts for advice on extinguishing graphite core reactor fires. A US expert in bone marrow transplants, Dr Robert Gale, was invited to help treat the worst-affected victims.

Slowly the Kremlin began to recognize that international uproar was inevitable. Moscow Communist Party chief Boris Yeltsin, later to become President of the Russian Federation, gave the first public hint of what was to come. 'It is serious, very serious,' he said. 'The cause apparently lies in human error. We are undertaking measures to make sure this doesn't happen again.'

One of the most urgent measures taken by the authorities was the complete evacuation of the 50,000 inhabitants of the nearby city of Pripyat, beginning the day after the disaster. It is still a ghost town today.

It took a week to extinguish the fire at the nuclear plant, and by then hundreds of soldiers and fire-fighters had received potentially lethal doses of radiation. Helicopters dropped tons of wet sand and lead on top of the burning reactor in an attempt to smother the flames. Boron, an element that soaks up radioactive neutrons, was also scattered around. Yet throughout the damage-limitation operation the Soviets seemed to have no clear planning strategy. Devoid of any better idea, they resorted to digging an enormous pit into which they bulldozed contaminated soil, bits of burned-out reactor and the clothes of the disaster team. This deadly cocktail of debris was then covered with 2 million cubic feet of concrete, later referred to as 'the sarcophagus'.

Inside the shattered heart of the building. It took weeks to extinguish the blaze.

Workmen wearing inadequate protective clothing attempted to decontaminate the building.

As snippets of intelligence information on the disaster trickled out, Western governments began to grow impatient. Nuclear experts were aghast at the shoddy way in which the Soviets had taken safety precautions. Had the doomed reactor been covered with a concrete outer shell – standard design in the West – much of the fire and radiation could have been contained. In an address to the American nation, President Ronald Reagan insisted: 'The Soviets owe the world an explanation. A full accounting of what happened at Chernobyl and what is happening now is the least the world community has a right to expect.'

Meanwhile the daunting task of evacuating 100,000 people living within an 18-mile radius of the plant continued. Within a few months the first legacies of Chernobyl were emerging: mutated calves and lambs, stillborn babies, blood disorders and deformed vegetation. Later, statisticians would discover the number of leukaemia cases in Minsk alone had doubled.

Ignoring world criticism, Moscow found suitable scapegoats in three off-duty Chernobyl workers who were rostered for night duty and were not even due to begin their shifts until the evening of 26 April. The three – plant director Viktor

(**Above**) Russia's Boris Yeltsin admitted: 'It is serious, very serious. The cause apparently lies in human error.'
America's Ronald Reagan demanded: 'The Soviets owe the world a full accounting of what happened at Chernobyl.'
(**Below**) The legacy of Chernobyl: children at a cancer hospital in Minsk.

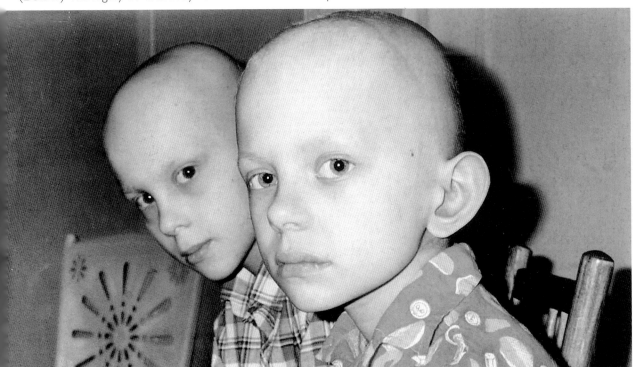

(**Opposite and above**) A fairground where no one ever plays … the contaminated area from which 100,000 people were evacuated after the explosion.

Bryukhanov, chief engineer Nikolai Fomin and his deputy Anatoly Dyatlov – justifiably proclaimed their innocence, but at their trial in July 1987 were found guilty of dereliction of duty and sentenced to ten years in a labour camp. In 2006, twenty years after that fateful day, Bryukhanov in a rare interview told of how the scientists had covered up the full truth:

> You need to understand the real causes of the disaster in order to know which direction you should develop alternative sources of energy. In this sense, Chernobyl has not taught anything to anyone… The scientists, the construction engineers, the prosecution experts, they all defended their professional interests and that was all. It was a tissue of lies that distracted us from the real cause of the accident.

Workmen must still wear protective clothing when at the site of the catastrophe.

The official estimate of casualties was a farce. Two people died immediately as a result of the blast and another twenty-nine died in hospital over the next few days. In addition, it was initially claimed, another 1,000 suffered sickness and there was the likelihood of 6,000 directly-attributable cancer deaths over the next 70 years. Shortly before the break-up of the Soviet Union, ex-President Mikhail Gorbachev admitted that the figures had been massaged. Experts still cannot agree on the death toll resulting from Chernobyl. A 1990 report to the UK government forecast that there would eventually be about 10,000 fatalities. However, environmental groups believe that the death toll could yet rise to 250,000.

Chapter Thirteen

Calamity in the Channel (1987)

It should have been just another hop across the English Channel for the car ferry *Herald of Free Enterprise*. Her 459 passengers regarded the four-hour voyage from Zeebrugge to Dover as no more risky than catching a bus to work. Their minds were on trivialities. Had they bought enough duty-free goods? Should they have a full fried supper? How long would the final drive home take? Many were travelling on a special £1 day-return ticket provided by one of Britain's mass-circulation daily newspapers, meaning that the vessel was operating at full capacity. As they settled into seats in the bars and restaurants, the last thing on their minds was the ship's safety. Weather forecasts for the evening of 6 March 1987 predicted slightly choppy seas, typical for the time of year.

At 6.05pm Captain David Lewry eased his 7,951-ton vessel away from Pier 12 and headed west. One of the Townsend Thoresen line's longest-serving skippers, he had made the crossing many times and knew the procedures off by heart. Among the strict rules to observe before sailing was the closing of the bow doors, through which the *Herald* had admitted her cargo of forty-seven lorries, three buses and eighty-one cars. Captain Lewry assumed that this had been done as he cast off the moorings. He could not see the bows from the bridge but he knew that a crew member would have been assigned responsibility for operating the doors. As a safety precaution, the first officer was also expected to double-check that they were closed.

Many masters were not happy with this system. For a start, they knew fears had been raised that the design of their ships was inherently unseaworthy. Ocean-going vessels are normally equipped with watertight bulkheads to seal off sections inside the hull. If there is a leak, flooding can often be confined to the area of damage. Car ferries, on the other hand, rely on vast open areas for quick and efficient parking. If water pours in, it is free to slosh around the vehicle decks, instantly destabilizing the ship. The fact that Townsend Thoresen captains recognized this danger is obvious from a memo sent to the crew of the *Herald*'s sister ship, the *Pride of Free Enterprise*, three years earlier. It read:

> Twice since going on the Zeebrugge run, this ship has sailed with the stern or bow doors open. No doubt this is caused by job/rank changes from the Calais

Shipping line Townsend Thoresen's cross-Channel ferry *Herald of Free Enterprise*.

run; however, all those named persons must see that the system is worked to make sure this dangerous situation does not occur. Give it your utmost attention.

In June 1985 another of the *Pride*'s skippers asked the fleet's managing director to install 'doors closed' indicators on the bridges of all vessels. This, he argued, would enable all captains to be absolutely certain they were putting to sea safely. The reply he got from one shore-based official was scathing: 'Do they need an indicator to tell them whether the deck storekeeper is awake and sober? My goodness.' The official would live to regret his words.

The seaman in charge of the doors as the *Herald* left Zeebrugge was Assistant Boatswain Mark Stanley. He was asleep in his bunk. The officer charged with ensuring he performed his duty was Chief Officer Leslie Sabel, who didn't check up. As a result, the doors stayed open. Twenty minutes into the voyage, just as the *Herald* left the shelter of Zeebrugge's 3-mile sea wall defence, the waves became large enough to lap over the open doors and into her hull. A night of terror had begun.

The seaman in charge of the ferry doors, Assistant Boatswain Mark Stanley, at the public inquiry.

There was panic on the main passenger decks as the ferry suddenly listed, partially righted herself and then teetered over again. In the first forty-five seconds of the disaster her hull had half-filled with water and within four minutes she had capsized, toppling onto her side like some mortally-wounded sea monster. She lay in barely 30ft of water, the whole of her starboard side clearly visible.

Dozens died in those first chaotic minutes, sucked down in the torrents that raged through the ship. Others drowned in the rest rooms or their private cabins. Screaming survivors flailed about in the blackness, unable to orientate themselves in the surreal environment that surrounded them. Stairs ran sideways while passageways turned into sheer pits dropping into an unforgiving, freezing sea. One eye-witness, Irish lorry driver Larry O'Brian, recalled how the only warning of impending disaster was when plates flew off the tables in the ship's restaurant:

> People were sucked out through portholes like you see in those movies about air disasters. They didn't have a chance. And the boat – well, when I was being taken off it and I looked back at it, it looked like something out of the Second World War that was hit with torpedoes.

One of the passengers travelling on the newspaper special-offer ticket was 30-year-old Andrew Simmons from Hertfordshire. He recalled:

> We were trapped for 20 or 30 minutes after the boat went over. Within a minute, it went from being upright to on its side with water gushing in down the stairs and corridors. I and my friend helped a little girl, who was only two or three years old, climb up with her father above the water. We were only rescued when people smashed the windows from outside and hauled us out to safety.

In those desperate hours, heroes would emerge performing the most unlikely deeds, like Londoner Andrew Parker who formed himself into a human bridge by stretching his body across the rising waters. Around 120 people crawled to safety over him and his bravery was later recognized with the George Medal. Equally heroic was Belgian naval frogman Lieutenant Guido Couwenbergh who was one of the first rescue workers to arrive. With little thought for his own safety, he managed to pull forty people out of the wreck, all of them numb with shock and cold. Couwenbergh later received the Queen's Gallantry Medal. One survivor, teenager Nicola Simpson from Hertfordshire, had a body temperature 25 degrees below normal, a state of hypothermia that meant she was clinically dead. Amazingly, she was resuscitated and made a full recovery. She owes her life to Belgian civilian diver Piet Lagast who smashed a thick sheet of glass to reach her, almost chopping off his hand in the process. He too was given the Queen's Gallantry Medal.

As the minutes ticked by, more and more rescue craft arrived on the scene. The British warships HMS *Glasgow* and HMS *Diomede* helped co-ordinate naval helicopters from Culdrose, Scotland, in combing waters around the wreck for signs of survivors. One chopper pilot said later: 'I could see black shapes bobbing in the water, arms splayed out like jellyfish. I knew they were dead.'

Meanwhile, hospitals in Zeebrugge were put on red alert to tackle a major disaster. Off-duty doctors and nurses were rounded up and requests for assistance were passed to other hospitals along the coast. Predictably, there were not enough beds to go round.

Back in England, the disaster was announced on the 9 o'clock news. Worried relatives began assembling at Dover docks to demand more information and found hordes of TV, radio and newspaper reporters already there waiting. In the fear and frustration of the moment, some of the journalists were attacked. When the full scale of the disaster struck home, it became clear that almost four in every ten passengers had died — a total of 193 victims, including almost 40 crew — and everyone else aboard needed hospital treatment. For dozens of survivors, the legacy of Zeebrugge would be a ceaselessly repeated nightmare. Years later, many continued to seek treatment for post-traumatic stress disorder.

(**Below**) The *Herald of Free Enterprise* lies on her side outside the Belgian port of Zeebrugge. (**Opposite**) A tug keeps the ferry under control as the waves wash through her decks.

Lifejackets that could have saved many lives hang down useless inside the ferry.

In July 1987 a twenty-nine-day inquiry conducted by Mr Justice Barry Sheen, Admiralty Judge of the High Court, concluded that the ship sank because neither Mr Stanley nor Mr Sabel did their jobs properly. Senior Master John Kirby was also criticized for his conduct. Ultimate responsibility, said the judge, rested with Captain Lewry. It was, after all, his ship. However, the criticism didn't end there. Justice Sheen was determined that Townsend Thoresen should not escape condemnation for the 'disease of sloppiness' that seemed to affect the entire company. Shore-based officials, he said, were guilty of 'staggering complacency' in failing to respond to the concerns of their ships' officers. The judge went on:

> By the autumn of 1986 the shore staff of the company were well aware of the possibility that one of their ships would sail with her stern or bow doors open. This topic has been discussed at length because it shows the attitude of the marine department [of Townsend Thoresen] to suggestions made by the masters.

Later, in October 1987, an inquest jury at Dover decided that all the dead had been unlawfully killed. A prosecution for manslaughter by gross negligence was mounted

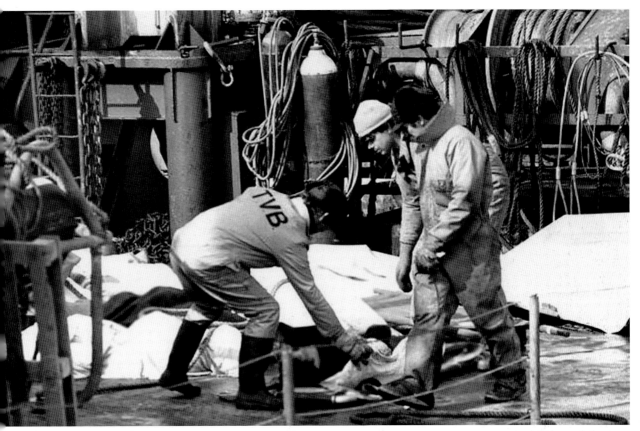

(**Above**) Rescue workers had the gruesome task of recovering the bodies of some of the 193 victims. (**Below**) The battered remains of cars and trucks as salvage work begins.

After being righted, the *Herald of Free Enterprise* was towed into harbour at Vlissingen in May 1987.

against Captain Lewry and six others but the case ended in acquittal. It was evident to everyone that the men would suffer for the rest of their lives. A manslaughter charge was also brought against the operating company, by then P&O European Ferries, and although that case also collapsed, it did set a precedent that 'corporate manslaughter' is admissible in English courts.

As for the *Herald* herself, having been righted by giant floating cranes, she was towed to Taiwan where, bolt by bolt, she was broken up in a dockside scrapyard, an ignoble end for an infamous ship.

Chapter Fourteen

Alaska's Toxic Tragedy (1989)

A few minutes after midnight on 24 March 1989 the 'unthinkable' happened. A giant oil tanker, the *Exxon Valdez*, struck Bligh Reef in the blackness of the Alaskan night and spewed into the icy sea more than 10 million gallons of crude oil. The damage to 1,300 miles of largely pristine coastline was devastating. At least 250,000 seabirds died, along with innumerable thousands of killer whales, seals, otters and even bald eagles, the national emblem of the United States.

Why had such a catastrophe been deemed 'unthinkable'? For decades the major players in the US oil market had dismissed the risk of environmental disaster as a statistical impossibility. As recently as 1987 a safety assessment by a consortium of these companies had reassuringly promised: 'It is highly unlikely that there will ever be a spill of any magnitude.' Yet only two months before the *Exxon Valdez* catastrophe, a relatively small discharge of 1,500 barrels had pushed the oil industry's fast-reaction clean-up team to its limits. Faced with the enormous Alaskan spillage, that team was now demonstrably out of its league.

The cause of the disaster that shamed Exxon, one of America's best-known corporate giants, had started the previous evening in the former Klondike Gold Rush town of Valdez, located at the head of a fjord on the eastern shore of Prince William Sound. Valdez was transformed into a boom town in the mid-1970s as the terminal for the Trans-Alaska pipeline from the newly-discovered Prudhoe Bay oilfield some 800 miles to the north. Valdez had done well out of the pipeline. A community that once lived desperately close to the poverty line had been inundated with new oil jobs and consequently bulging pay packets. Thus, on this particular night, the atmosphere in the town's Pipeline Club was thick with tobacco smoke and the fumes of alcohol. It was the kind of place beloved by seamen and oilmen and on the evening of 23 March 1989 both trades were well represented when Captain Joseph Hazelwood walked in with two of his officers to down a few beers and vodkas.

Hazelwood was a familiar face at the Pipeline Club. The 42-year-old skipper of the supertanker *Exxon Valdez* earned his living transporting millions of barrels of Alaskan crude oil to the ever-thirsty refineries of California and Texas. He enjoyed a drink

The size of three football pitches … tugs guide the mighty *Exxon Valdez* through Prince William Sound.

whenever he put into Valdez, especially if he was facing a long trip. True, the Exxon Company had a strict rule banning consumption of alcohol during the four hours before a voyage but Hazelwood liked to interpret that flexibly. After all, he spent most of his time on the Valdez-West Coast run and he knew the waters of the Sound like the roads around his home on Long Island, New York. He did not regard the waters as particularly difficult to navigate. However, he would live to regret every gulp of the 'three or four vodkas' he admitted putting away that evening, for the accident that was to follow left him portrayed as a captain drunk in charge of his ship. It was an unfair label but one the public easily identified with and, while he was subsequently acquitted of operating a ship while intoxicated, it stuck.

Captain Joseph Hazelwood, skipper of the *Exxon Valdez.*

The Trans-Alaska pipeline runs 800 miles from the Prudhoe Bay oilfield to the port of Valdez.

At 8.00pm Hazelwood and his drinking companions, Third Mate Gregory Cousins and Able Seaman Robert Kagan, were back aboard the *Exxon Valdez*. At 9.10pm the 211,469-ton vessel slipped her moorings to begin the voyage to Long Beach, California. It was an hour earlier than her scheduled sailing time but the US Coast Guard Vessel Traffic Control Center had given the all-clear. For the next two hours and twenty minutes, harbour pilot William Murphy would have control, navigating the ship through the initial shallow sea lane littered with jagged rocks. Later Murphy would tell investigators that he smelled alcohol on the skipper's breath that night but that his demeanour did not indicate that he was intoxicated.

Shortly after Murphy left the ship to return to port on a launch, Hazelwood made two course changes. He was concerned about ice showing on the radar and asked traffic control if he could switch to the clearer inbound sea lane. The controller gave permission, assuring him there were no inbound ships in the vicinity.

Hazelwood planned to clear the ice below Busby Island before heading south-west in a narrow passage between the submerged rocks of Bligh Reef and another major ice floe. It was a tricky manoeuvre but not one the captain pondered over. In fact, he was so confident that he planned to hand the entire operation over to Third Mate Cousins and retire to his cabin to sleep.

Hazelwood's style of captaincy was a 'hands-off' approach. He was a highly-skilled master and believed that the best way to teach his juniors the ropes was to delegate responsibility. He had few worries about 38-year-old Cousins' competence. In a staff evaluation report the previous year, he rated his third mate as having 'excellent navigational skills', though 'only average knowledge of ship-handling characteristics'.

In the half hour between 11.30pm and midnight, Hazelwood made two of his most questionable decisions. The first was to give the order 'load program up', an instruction to activate the ship's computer program responsible for regulating build-up to full sea speed. The second was to engage the auto-pilot. With considerable ice about, many masters would have thought twice before relinquishing manual control, especially when a junior such as Cousins was watch officer.

Was it possible that fondness for drink affected the captain's judgement? Or was Hazelwood such a talented mariner that he could not imagine the problems less gifted men might face? From the moment Hazelwood left the bridge, just before midnight, Gregory Cousins' watch became one big problem. He had been instructed to make a right-hand turn back into the outbound sea lane after reaching a navigational point near Busby Island. Yet, unaccountably, Cousins waited six minutes too long before starting the turn. As a result, the tanker was a mile further ahead than she should have been. Had Cousins been able to look at the ship's RAYCAS radar, the disaster that was about to unfold might have been averted. However, the radar was turned off due to a fault that had left it disabled for more than a year, a snag of which Exxon management were aware but deemed too costly to fix and operate.

At six minutes past midnight, the ship had moved to a course of 247 degrees, a major change that helmsman Robert Kagan felt should be corrected. He tried to slow the swing before Cousins ordered: 'Hard right rudder'. By now, both men could see they were way off line and Cousins made a desperate phone call to his captain. 'I think we are in serious trouble,' he said.

Hazelwood already knew it. A few seconds earlier, he had felt a terrible juddering from the bowels of the ship. He guessed they had run onto the reef and his principal fear as he sprinted to the bridge was that if part of the hull slipped she could break her back. A fully-laden crude carrier the size of three football pitches would be at the mercy of the waves.

As the crisis unfolded, Hazelwood produced a textbook response. By carefully varying his engine power, he was able to keep the *Exxon Valdez* tight to the reef, ensuring her stability. If drink had given him a fuzzy head, the prospect of a giant oil

Booms that were floated around the stricken tanker arrived late and failed to stem the spill.

slick now brought his thoughts sharply back into focus. Below water, the ship's hull had sustained rents up to 16ft long. Eight of her fifteen holds had been penetrated and the first of 40,000 tons of her viscous black cargo was leaking into the seas of one of the world's most environmentally sensitive coastlines. In the days ahead, 10 million gallons would be lost.

The damage was irreparable, largely because it took ten hours for the industry's dedicated oil spillage rescue teams to reach the scene. When they arrived, they had no booms – vital if a slick is to be contained – and their detergents proved useless because the sea was too calm. Attempts to burn off the oil proved a waste of time, and the US Coast Guard, required by law to have a vessel on hand for damage-control operations, transparently failed in its duty. Its tiny fleet was cruising 2,000 miles away off San Francisco.

By Sunday, 26 March, the slick covered a massive 900 square miles. It polluted the hundreds of remote, rocky coves that run the length of Prince William Sound. An estimated 86,000 birds, 1,000 sea otters, 25,000 fish, 200 seals and dozens of beavers were all killed.

Some beaches had to be treated seven times with detergents and other chemicals. Environmental scientist Paul Millard said: 'The spill happened in almost the worst place possible. The jagged coast of Prince William Sound is dotted with innumerable

Smaller sister ship the *Exxon Baton Rouge* attempts to offload crude oil from the *Exxon Valdez*.

coves and inlets where the spilled oil collected and stayed for months, killing young fish that spawn in the shallows.'

America was in uproar at news of the incident, portrayed by the media as the worst on record. In fact, the *Exxon Valdez* slick ranks only tenth in the league of oil tanker disasters. It was but a seventh the size of the *Amoco Cadiz* leak that hit north-west France in March 1977, and it was only an eighth as big as the world's worst oil

(**Above**) Desperate efforts were made to clean the rocky coves with detergent and chemicals. (**Below**) A dead whale: just one victim among the dreadful toll of wildlife.

tanker spillage caused by the collision of the *Aegean Captain* and the *Atlantic* Empress off Tobago in the Caribbean in 1979. However, its effect on the oil industry and the loss of American prestige as a nation capable of handling such an environmental crisis was deeply shaming as the catastrophe was played out on worldwide television over the months ahead.

Captain Hazelwood was summarily dismissed. Exxon said that blood alcohol tests taken nine hours after the ship grounded proved he had been drinking in breach of company rules. In any case, he had already been tried and convicted by the media. Newspapers told how in 1985 he had spent twenty-eight days in a drying-out clinic near New York. The treatment followed his conviction for drunken driving the previous year. Hazelwood, it was also claimed, had a reputation among the *Exxon* crew for livening up long voyages with parties.

If Exxon hoped that Hazelwood would prove a handy scapegoat, it was wrong. Later inquiries concluded that he acted with honour and initiative after the accident. Moreover, they expressed concern about the fatigue of his crew. *Exxon Valdez* was one of the largest vessels afloat, yet her manning had been reduced in recent years from twenty-four to twenty crew members, who worked twelve- to fourteen-hour shifts plus overtime. The implications for the company were huge. Full-page newspaper adverts were taken out urging a consumer boycott of its products. Petrol stations across the country stood empty following accusations that the company had

After several name changes, the *Exxon Valdez* was dismantled for scrap in India in 2012.

not adequately responded to the leak. Exxon President Frank Iarossi was forced to promise a hefty $1 billion to assist with the clean-up exercise and compensate fishermen for their lost livelihoods.

So who eventually paid the price of the human errors that led to the *Exxon Valdez* disaster? The cost, as evaluated by a US federal judge, was $5 billion in damages ordered to be paid by the Exxon oil company, the largest such award in American history. The sum was whittled down in subsequent appeals to a tenth of that figure. As a result of the disaster, newer tankers were designed with double hulls as a safety feature to restrict oil leaks. The *Exxon Valdez* herself was repaired and, renamed the *SeaRiver Mediterranean*, continued to work as an oil tanker, although barred from returning to Alaska. Following further name changes, she was finally dismantled for scrap in India in 2012.

As for Captain Joseph Hazelwood, he was cleared of being drunk in charge of his ship after witnesses at his 1990 trial testified that he was perfectly sober at the time of the accident. Convicted of the lesser charge of 'negligent discharge of oil', he was fined $50,000 and sentenced to 1,000 hours of community service. He was to have been made to help with the clean-up of the oil spill but, due to lengthy appeals, he ended up serving out his time clearing rubbish from Alaskan roadsides and serving in a soup kitchen. He offered a 'heartfelt apology' to the people of Alaska but claimed he had been wrongly blamed for the disaster.

Chapter Fifteen

Ferry Families' Icy End (1994)

The sinking of the MS *Estonia* with the loss of 852 passengers and crew was Europe's worst peacetime disaster since the Second World War. After the horrors of Zeebrugge, nobody really believed that such a tragedy could happen again. The fact that it did once more called into question the basic design of ro-ro (roll-on/roll-off) vehicle ferries.

For those with no knowledge of marine engineering, it seemed incredible that such a bulky vessel could sink inside forty-five minutes. The problem was that once water breached the cargo decks, there were no bulkheads that could be sealed off. Waves were free to run the length of the ship's interior, destroying her balance.

Perhaps the most shocking aspect of the *Estonia* disaster was that for dozens of passengers death may have come agonizingly slowly. Experts suspect that some victims may have survived for hours, trapped in air pockets in the ship as she rested on the seabed, hoping against hope that help would come and, finally, succumbing to the unremitting numbing cold. In the history of disasters at sea, the last voyage of the *Estonia* is among the grimmest chapters.

Yet until the moment of her doom, everything about the overnight voyage across the Baltic Sea from Tallinn, Estonia to Stockholm, Sweden had seemed perfectly normal, apart from a slight listing to starboard due to a full load that was badly distributed. The *Estonia* was carrying 989 people, of whom 186 were crew and 803 were passengers. By the early hours of that Wednesday morning, 28 September 1994, most of the latter, mainly businessmen, day-trippers and shoppers, were already tucked up in bed. In the Baltic Bar, however, the Henry Goy dance band was still banging out Elvis Presley and Beatles numbers for the largely middle-aged night owls. They carried on until 1.00am when the rolling of the ship in gale-force winds (7–8 on the Beaufort scale) became too much.

A few die-hard drinkers made their way to the nearby Pub Admiral for a nightcap. There was still a chance to try out the karaoke machine. One of the groups taking the microphone had been attending an on-board conference run by Swedish oil executive Tomas Grunde. The delegates regarded the event as a perk and were making

(**Above**) The ferry *Estonia* which sank with the loss of 852 passengers and crew. (**Below**) The *Estonia*, seen here at port with bow doors open. All the evidence pointed to a fault with them.

the most of every moment. Grunde, aged 43, who was to be one of only 137 survivors, recalled what happened next:

> When we came to the end there was a big bang at the front and the ship started
> to lean a little. Some were afraid, others laughed. Myself, I did not react. Then
> came another bang, still worse than the first, and the ship started really to lean
> over. I shot over the dance floor and hit my forehead on a chair or table. A friend
> helped me to get up, asking how I was feeling. From that moment I had only one
> thought: I had to get out.

Another reveller, Altti Hakanpää from Finland, believed that his decision to take a
late-night drink saved his life. He recalled:

> If I had been asleep in my cabin I would, without doubt, be dead now. I was just
> about to have a drink when I felt the boat list dangerously. I realised something
> was wrong. I rushed to take the elevator to the top deck and the liferafts. I was
> panic-stricken. I watched as the *Estonia* sank beneath the waves. It was terrible. It
> all happened so quickly. Around ten minutes passed between the time the ship
> first began to list and when it disappeared.

It seems the *Estonia* began shipping water soon after 1.00am. Yet, perplexingly, it was
not until 1.26am that the bridge sent out its first and only distress signal: 'Mayday,
Mayday. We have a list of 20 to 30 degrees. Blackout. Mayday.' Why this SOS was not
transmitted earlier and why no attempt was made to muster passengers before the
situation became critical remained two of the key questions for investigators.

As the ship went down, the pathetic cries of the dying filled the air. One survivor,
named in newspaper reports as Heidi Auvinen, aged 31, recalled:

> I was thrown into the sea and tried to find a place in a lifeboat. I grabbed a rope
> attached to one of the lifeboats. With great effort and despite waves several
> metres high I was able to drag myself aboard. The raging sea looked terrible,
> with corpses floating in the water, lifeboats, abandoned clothing. I heard distant
> cries for help, groaning. The memory will haunt me for ever.

Andrus Maidre, a 19-year-old Estonian on a pleasure cruise with friends, witnessed
the most pathetic and heartbreaking sight of all. 'Some old people had already given
up hope and were just sitting there crying,' he said. 'I also stepped over children who
were wailing and holding on to the railing.' Among the first ships to answer the
Mayday was the ferry *Isabella*. One of its passengers, Swede Hemming Eriksson,
painted a dreadful picture of the carnage that confronted him:

> There were hundreds of bodies that were bobbing up and down in the sea.
> Many were dressed only in underwear and life vests. Some of them moved, so

you could see they were living, but we had no chance to bring them up in the heavy sea. The worst was when the bodies got sucked into the propellers.

A full-scale emergency was not declared until 2.30am with the *Mariella* being the first ferry to reach the scene. Swedish and Finnish helicopters did not arrive until half an hour later to begin winching people from the sea. While the Swedes transported the survivors to shore, the Finnish helicopters set them down by landing their aircraft on the decks of rescue ships. Despite being the most perilous part of the whole mission, one spectacularly successful helicopter crew saved forty-four people; more than the number saved by all the rescue ships combined.

So what was the cause of the *Estonia*'s catastrophic sinking? All the evidence pointed to a fault in the bow doors, designed to open and close for the loading of vehicles. Bow doors were blamed in the *Herald of Free Enterprise* disaster at Zeebrugge. However, whereas the error that doomed the *Herald* was down to a sleeping crewman and lax on-board safety systems, it was not immediately obvious why the *Estonia*'s doors had failed.

One theory was that they had been smashed open by the intense battering-ram action of the sea, hence the loud metallic bangs that some passengers reported

A search-and-rescue helicopter hovers over an empty life-raft.

(**Above**) An upturned lifeboat from the *Estonia*. (**Below**) Relatives of ferry passengers wait mournfully at Tallinn harbour, Estonia, for news of their loved ones.

hearing. Rune Petterson, an expert in marine hydraulics, had carried out work on the German-built *Estonia* in 1988 when she was named the *Sally Viking*, one of her several identities before being chartered by an Estonian company in 1991. Petterson pointed out that the ferry operated with both the bow 'visor' and the vehicle ramp, which forms an inner door when raised, being locked in place by the same hydraulic system. He said:

> A leak in a cylinder or valve could have made the holding pressure sink, thereby making one or more locks lose their grip on the visor. The gaskets in the big lifting cylinders have to take the full pressure and then they may have been torn away from their fastenings. The result would be a loosening of the locks on the inner door as well, allowing the sea to drive into a narrow opening. If this was indeed the case, the force of water entering the ship would be almost incomprehensible. A gap of 1 square metre, and water entering at a speed of 10 metres a second, would mean that in 1 second 10 tonnes of water would have got in. In the space of a minute, the ship would have taken on 600 tonnes.

The Estonian government was reluctant to accept this theory, believing it compromised both the integrity of the ship and her crew. Johannes Johanson, managing director of the ferry's owners, Estline, pointed out that forty old wartime sea mines had been found near the island of Osmussaar, which lay many miles to the south-west of the *Estonia*'s last known position. His hypothesis of an explosion was backed by the ferry's third engineer, Margus Treu. He said: 'I was in the engine room and then I heard two or three strong blows, as though the ship had sailed into a wave. But these blows shook the whole ship so it was not a natural sound. This was an alien sound.'

As realization of the disaster began to dawn in Estonia and Sweden, dozens of towns and villages were thrown into mourning. Lindesberg, some 40 miles north of Stockholm, lost twenty-two women, all mothers with children aged under 18. The suburb of Uppsala lost 26 of its court officials who had been on a fact-finding mission to Estonia, and at Jönköping, south of Stockholm, 400 people packed the local church to mourn for 13 pupils and their 2 teachers who had been on a Bible school outing. Of the 989 passengers and crew, only 137 survived. The Swedes lost 501 nationals, Estonia 285, Latvia 17, Russia 11, Finland 10, Norway 6, Denmark 5, Germany 5, Lithuania 3 and Morocco 2, with Belarus, Canada, France, the Netherlands, Nigeria, Ukraine and the United Kingdom each losing 1 national.

The pain of the mourners was tangible. For the survivors it must have been unbearable. Not only had they watched hundreds of young lives snuffed out, but they had been totally helpless to act. Many felt guilty for being alive. Symptoms of post-traumatic stress disorder would soon start to appear.

The bow doors recovered from the sea bed.

One of the rescued passengers was 29-year-old Kent Härstedt, a student from Lund University, Sweden. He had rushed from his cabin when the first blow struck the ship and had found himself on deck alongside another student, 20-year-old Sara Hedrenius. Härstedt introduced himself using his full name, an odd formality in laid-back Swedish culture. They both believe that chance meeting on the edge of disaster kept them alive. Together they clawed their way to what had become the top side of the ship. Then, before jumping, they agreed to meet in a Stockholm restaurant for dinner the following week. Both of them kept the date. As Härstedt put it: 'Somewhere in this chaos we have to encourage each other.'